CITIZEN
PAINE

CITIZEN PAINE

Thomas Paine's Thoughts on Man, Government, Society, and Religion

Compiled and Edited by
JOHN P. KAMINSKI

A MADISON HOUSE BOOK
ROWMAN & LITTLEFIELD PUBLISHERS, INC.
Lanham • Boulder • New York • Oxford

A MADISON HOUSE BOOK

Rowman & Littlefield Publishers, Inc.
4720 Boston Way, Lanham, Maryland 20706
www.rowmanlittlefield.com

12 Hid's Copse Road
Cumnor Hill, Oxford OX2 9JJ, England

ISBN 0-7425-2088-9 (alk. paper)

Printed in the United States of America

∞™ The paper used in this publication meets the minimum requirements of American National Standard for Information Sciences—Permanence of Paper for Printed Library Materials, ANSI/NISO Z.39.48–1992.

For Laura

CONTENTS

PREFACE

ix

CHRONOLOGY

xi

INTRODUCTION

1

THE WORDS OF PAINE

35

INDEX

249

PREFACE

While indexing the Library of America's *Thomas Paine: Collected Writings* (1995) I realized that there was a "Citizen Paine" in these writings to match my *Citizen Jefferson* (1994). I used the Library of America edition and Philip S. Foner's two-volume *Complete Writings of Thomas Paine* (1945) in searching Paine's writings. I profited greatly from Professor Foner's introduction; Crane Brinton's essay on Paine in the *Dictionary of American Biography*; David Freeman Hawke's *Paine* (1974); John Keane's biography of Paine, *Tom Paine: A Political Life* (1995); Eric Foner's *Tom Paine and Revolutionary America* (1976); and Carl Van Doren's introduction to the Modern Library edition of *The Writings of Thomas Paine*.

I am grateful to Richard Leffler, Gregory M. Britton, and Michael E. Stevens who have read the manuscript and made thoughtful suggestions. This book is dedicated to my daughter Laura in whom I see a great deal of Thomas Paine's spirit and vitality.

THOMAS PAINE
CHRONOLOGY

1737–1809

1737   Born January 29 in Thetford, Norfolk, England.

1743   Begins attending grammar school in Thetford.

1748   Leaves school and begins apprenticeship with father.

1756   Enlists on privateer *Terrible* but does not serve.

1757   Enlists on privateer *King of Prussia*.

1759   Marries Mary Lambert.

1760   Wife and baby die.

1762   Appointed excise tax collector.

1765   Dismissed from excise service.

1766   Moves to London and teaches in private academy.

1768   Reappointed to excise service in Lewes, Sussex, England.

1770   Runs tobacconist shop and expands it into grocery.

1771   Marries Elizabeth Ollive.

1774   Dismissed from excise service. Grocery business fails. Separates from wife. Leaves England for America. Arrives in Philadelphia on November 30.

1775   Becomes editor of the *Pennsylvania Magazine*. Battles of Lexington and Concord on April 19. Begins writing *Common Sense*.

1776   Publishes *Common Sense* in January. Publishes "The Forester" series of essays. Congress declares independence and approves Declaration on July 4. Paine writes *The American Crisis*, Number I.

1777   Continues writing *The American Crisis* into 1783. Appointed secretary to Committee for Foreign Affairs.

1778   Franco-American treaties signed in February.

1779   Resigns as secretary to Committee for Foreign Affairs. Refuses offer to write for French government. Appointed clerk of Pennsylvania Assembly on November 2.

1780   Resigns as clerk of Pennsylvania Assembly in November. Publishes *Public Good* in December.

1781   Travels to France with John Laurens, February–August. Battle of Yorktown, October 19.

1782   Secretly agrees to write for Congress and army. Publishes *Letter Addressed to the Abbé Raynal* in August.

1784   Receives compensation from France and New York.

1785   Elected to the American Philosophical Society. Receives compensation from Pennsylvania and Congress. Begins work on iron bridge.

1786   Publishes *Dissertations on Government*.

1787   Sails for France to get endorsements for his bridge, April 26.

1791   Publishes *Rights of Man*, Part I, in mid-March.

1792   Publishes *Rights of Man*, Part II, in February. Given honorary French citizenship on August 26. Elected to the National Convention by Calais on September 6.

1793   Opposes execution of Louis XVI. Arrested and imprisoned on December 28.

1794   Publishes *Age of Reason*, Part I, in January. Released from prison on November 4.

1795   Publishes *Age of Reason*, Part II, and *Dissertation on First Principles of Government*.

1796   Excerpt from Paine's letter to Washington published in Philadelphia *Aurora*.

1797	Publishes letter to Washington as a pamphlet and *Agrarian Justice*.
1802	Returns to United States.
1803	Returns to New York.
1809	Dies June 8; buried next day in New Rochelle, N.Y.
1819	William Cobbett exhumes Paine's remains, which are sent to England for a memorial. Remains are lost.

INTRODUCTION

Thomas Paine was the quintessential revolutionary. No other person captured so well the explosiveness of the last quarter of the eighteenth century. In 1805 John Adams, long a critic of Paine, satirically condemned the labeling of the era as the Age of Reason—the title of Paine's last major work.

> I am willing you should call this the Age of Frivolity . . . and would not object if you had named it the Age of Folly, Vice, Frenzy, Brutality, Daemons, Buonaparte, Tom Paine, or the Burning Brand from the Bottomless Pit, or anything but the Age of Reason. I know not whether any man in the world has had more influence on its inhabitants or affairs for the last thirty years than Tom Paine. . . . Call it then the Age of Paine.

Paine would have liked that; he was even more pleased with the name that stuck—the Age of Reason.

Thomas Paine was a complex man. Each of the fifty biographers since his death in 1809 has failed to unveil the full person. Because he will always be different things to different people, it is unlikely we shall ever obtain a completely persuasive biography of this enigmatic man. Joel Barlow, one of Paine's closest friends, was perhaps right when he wrote that Paine's "own writings are his best life." Taking Barlow's advice in this selection of Paine's writings, I attempt to identify the genius and the madness that was Thomas Paine.

1

Paine was a paradox. He turned a life of abysmal failure into phenomenal success, only to die pathetically lonely and neglected. He was a tolerant man of good will who lived every day as a rabid partisan. A pensive philosopher, he was ever the zealot driven to action. A gentle man of peace, he regularly wrote sedition and inspired men to take up arms in the cause of liberty. He came to be a symbol of rebellion and civil unrest, yet he was an ardent opponent of insurrection and a staunch advocate of law and order. He refused to profit financially from his God-given talents as a writer, yet he felt betrayed when his country refused to reward him financially for his "selfless" services. A deeply religious man, he was condemned as an atheist and blasphemer. He advocated harmony but lived a dissolute, disheveled life. He fervently sought the peace, stability, and enjoyment of a quiet life, but was continually immersed in scandal, conflict, and the vicissitudes of war. Though an eternal optimist, he was also a skeptic. He made friends easily, but lost them with even greater facility. A fervent spokesman for limited government, he was a sincere proponent of social welfare programs for the poor, the infirm, and the aged. Paine was a citizen of three countries, yet truly a man without a country—although to his own way of thinking, he was a citizen of the world.

* * *

Thomas Paine was born in 1737 in Thetford, England, an old, impoverished market town in the east coast county of Norfolk. A forbidding three-story, black-flint jail dominated the landscape. From his family's cottage, young Tom could view the town's gallows atop an ominous hill called the Wilderness, where every month prisoners convicted of petty thefts were hanged. The aristocratic dukes of Grafton, who ruled with lordly patronage, controlled Norfolk and wreaked swift vengeance on anyone who questioned their prerogatives. Their abuse of power had a strong impact on the impressionable youngster.

Joseph Paine, Tom's father, was a practicing Quaker until the Friends expelled him for marrying Frances Cocke, an Anglican. The couple's two children, Tom and his younger sister, Elizabeth, who died within seven months of her birth, were baptized in St. Cuthbert's Anglican Church. Despite his expulsion, Joseph Paine encouraged his son to attend Quaker meetings as well as Anglican services. As the self-righteousness of both congregations tugged at him, Tom developed a spirit of tolerance and eventually turned his back on formal religion.

When Tom was seven, his father sent him to Thetford Grammar School where he received an "English education" concentrating on arithmetic and writing and eschewing the ancient languages so often taught in that era. Later Paine wrote that he "did not learn Latin, not only because I had no inclination to learn languages, but because of the objection the Quakers have against the books in which the language is taught. But this did not prevent me from being acquainted with the subjects of all the Latin books used in the school."

Paine's father removed him after five years in school, and young Tom worked as his father's apprentice learning to become a staymaker for women's corsets. After he served his full seven-year apprenticeship, it became obvious that the family business could not support both father and son. Consequently, at the age of twenty, Paine ran off in 1756 and signed on board Captain William Death's privateer *Terrible* during the early fighting of the Seven Years' War. Before Paine left on his first voyage, however, his father located him and convinced him not to fight. The *Terrible*, without Paine aboard, lost over ninety percent of its crew in its first battle.

Paine resumed work as a staymaker in London, but in January 1757 he signed on to another privateer. During its six-month cruise, the *King of Prussia* captured a half-dozen vessels. Paine's share of the prize money was about £30—enough to support himself in London for the next nine months. During this time Paine met the famous Benjamin Franklin and read extensively in mathematics and science. He regularly attended lectures on astronomy and nature, and he purchased scientific apparatus. Soon he became enthralled with the Newtonian concept of a well-ordered universe and lamented that the logic and symmetry of the physical world was absent in society and government.

By the spring of 1758 Paine had spent all his prize money and returned to staymaking in Kent, seventy miles southeast of London. Eighteen months later he married Mary Lambert, an orphaned waiting woman. Within a year, Paine's business failed and his wife and baby died in childbirth.

After fourteen months of applications, tests, and waiting, Paine received an appointment as a collector of the excise tax. A promotion followed in August 1764, but a year later he was fired because of irregularities in his books. Penniless, he returned to staymaking. While awaiting word about his reinstatement in the excise service, Paine taught reading and writing in London at an academy for children of artisans. Finally, in February 1768 he received an appointment as an exciseman in Lewes, a town of about 5,000 people in the southeastern county of Sussex.

Although he created the usual enemies expected of a tax collector, Paine became a popular figure in Lewes. He joined a club that met weekly and honed his debating and writing skills on the issues of the day. While in Lewes, Paine lived with the family of Samuel Ollive, a Quaker tobacconist. After Ollive's death in 1769, Paine, out of propriety, found other living accommodations. In addition to his excise service, he assisted Ollive's widow and daughter Elizabeth in running the tobacco shop and expanded the store to include groceries. In March 1771, Paine married Elizabeth. He now had someone to care for his needs, but it was a marriage of convenience that was never consummated, and the newlyweds were incompatible.

Not long after the marriage, at the urging of his superiors in the excise service, Paine took up the cause of his fellow excisemen in a pamphlet and a petition to Parliament asking for higher pay. His efforts to unionize the excisemen failed miserably, and in April 1773 he was once again fired from the tax service. A year later Paine's marriage and business both failed. He declared bankruptcy, and he and Elizabeth were legally separated.

Faced with one failure after another, Paine decided to migrate to America. He received letters of introduction from Benjamin Franklin to Franklin's son-in-law, Richard Bache, a Philadelphia merchant, and to Franklin's son, William, royal governor of New Jersey. With a £35 settlement from his wife, Paine took first-class passage aboard the London packet bound for Philadelphia. The eight-week voyage was another disaster as Paine along with most of the other passengers came down with typhus. On November 30,

1774, the packet docked in Philadelphia and Paine, too sick to walk, was carried ashore. After six weeks of care by Franklin's friends, Paine visited Richard Bache, hoping to teach school or give private lessons in geography.

During his convalescence, Paine wrote an essay entitled "Dialogue Between General Wolfe and General Gage in a Wood near Boston," which was published in the *Pennsylvania Journal* on January 4, 1775. The essay was amazingly American—no one guessed it was written by a recent immigrant. In this imaginary dialogue between Thomas Gage, the new military governor of Massachusetts, and the ghost of General James Wolfe, who was killed in the Battle of Quebec in 1759, Paine alluded to the Intolerable Acts as Parliament's attempt to deprive Americans of their liberty. Americans, Paine wrote, cease to be British subjects when they cease to be governed by rulers of their own choice. "This is the essence of liberty and of the British constitution." Thus, a year and a half before the Declaration of Independence and ten weeks before the battles of Lexington and Concord, Paine pointed to independence. Inexplicably, the new immigrant conceived of a separate American identity well before most Americans.

In January 1775 Paine met Robert Aitken, a Scottish immigrant printer/bookseller, who was beginning a new monthly magazine. Aitken offered Paine the job of editor. Paine accepted the post and wrote about twenty percent of the content of the new *Pennsylvania Magazine or United States Monthly Museum*. At first he followed the apolitical policy established by Aitken, but after Lexington and Concord, Paine became an ardent revolutionary. His nonpolitical prose was plodding, but his attacks on British policy came alive. Subscriptions skyrocketed from 600 to 1,500, and the *Pennsylvania Magazine* became the most popular periodical printed in America. The collaboration between Paine and Aitken lasted but six months as their egos and their failure to agree on an acceptable salary created a widening rift.

Aitken also had trouble getting enough copy from Paine to fill the magazine by its publication deadline. In his *History of Printing in America*, Isaiah Thomas remembered a story told him by Aitken.

On one of the occasions, when Paine had neglected to supply the materials for the Magazine, within a short time of the day of publication, Aitken went to his [Paine's] lodgings, and complained of his neglecting to fulfill his contract. Paine heard him patiently, and coolly answered, "You shall have them in time." Aitken expressed some doubts on the subject, and insisted on Paine's accompanying him and proceeding immediately to business, as the workmen were waiting for copy. He accordingly went home with Aitken, and was soon seated at the table with the necessary apparatus, which always included a glass, and a decanter of brandy. Aitken remarked, "he would never write without *that*." The first glass put him in a train of thinking; Aitken feared the second would disqualify him, or render him untractable; but it only illuminated his intellectual system; and when he had swallowed the third glass, he wrote with great rapidity, intelligence, and precision; and his ideas appeared to flow faster than he could commit them to paper. What he penned from the inspiration of the brandy, was perfectly fit for the press without any alteration, or correction.

Paine spent less time on the magazine and increasingly more time writing inflammatory pieces for newspapers. Several essays criticized Great Britain for importing slaves from Africa into the New World. In one such essay signed "Humanus," printed in the *Pennsylvania Journal* in mid-October 1775, Paine predicted that God would punish the British for their sins and "will finally separate America from Britain. Call it independence or what you will, if it is the cause of God and humanity it will go on." America would soon be "a people *dependent only upon*" God. Again, Paine outpaced most Americans by appealing for independence.

Paine's antislavery writings helped to promote a friendship with Dr. Benjamin Rush, a lifelong reformer, who by 1772 had already publicly denounced slavery and the slave trade. Soon, with Rush's encouragement, Paine began a series of three newspaper essays on independence. By the end of September 1775, Paine brought the draft of his opening essay to Rush. "From time to time," Rush wrote in his autobiography, Paine "called at my house, and read to me every chapter." Rush suggested revisions, including changing the title from "Plain Truth" to "Common Sense." Paine soon abandoned the newspaper format in favor of a more extensive pamphlet publication. By early December, the finished manuscript was hand copied and sent to Benjamin Franklin, David Rittenhouse, and Samuel Adams. All enthusiastically supported publication. On January 10, 1776, the pamphlet, seventy-nine pages, was published anonymously "like an orphan to shift for itself." Rumors spread that Franklin, Rush, or John or Samuel Adams was the author. Soon, however, the author made sure that his identity was revealed, and it was reported that Paine had "Genius in his Eyes."

Common Sense faced a formidable task. Paine had to destroy all of the political paradigms of his day—monarchy, balanced government, complex government, mercantilism, the excellence of the British constitution, America as part of the British Empire, and the benefits and practicability of reconciliation. Americans had lived amicably under monarchy within the British Empire for some one hundred and fifty years, and Great Britain had no intention of giving up its North American colonies. Paine had to convince Americans to abandon their familial connection, their security under the British constitution, and the glory they shared with the mother country. He asked a band of loosely connected colonists, many of whom disliked each other, to declare war against the mightiest nation in the world. Failure to win that war would mean subjugation, loss of property, and death as traitors. If independence could be achieved, he argued that America should abandon monarchy and adopt a republican government—a form of government that had always been thought of as unstable and subject to political, social, and economic chaos. The anarchy of republicanism, so the argument went, always led to the rise of a dictator who promised stability and benevolence. Stability would indeed be restored but benevolence would soon disappear to be replaced by tyranny.

Common Sense argued that Great Britain had done little to help colonize America. In fact, British policy thwarted immigration to the New World and stifled economic development. The colonists owed allegiance to no one but themselves. They knew what was best for themselves, far better than some far-off ignorant and insensitive monarch ill-served by corrupt ministers and a Parliament bent on ruling America as a conquered people. Americans should immediately declare their independence because American liberty at that very moment was threatened under British rule. Reconciliation would only delay the inevitable retaliation by a vindicative king and Parliament. Independence would unify the colonies and secure French and Spanish assistance.

Paine boldly asserted that hereditary monarchy was inherently contrary to the laws of nature. Only through independence could America achieve its destiny under a republican form of government where men could govern themselves. America would serve as an example for the rest of the world. "The cause of America," he wrote in *Common Sense*, "is in a great measure the cause of all mankind." Paine, in one sentence, escalated the colonies' struggle for liberty into a crusade for all of mankind. *Common Sense* admitted that these ideas might seem strange at first,

> but like all other steps which we have already passed over, will in a little time become familiar and agreeable: and until an independence is declared, the continent will feel itself like a man who continues putting off some unpleasant business from day to day, yet knows it must be done, hates to set about it, wishes it over, and is continually haunted with the thoughts of its necessity.

Because none of this would amount to anything unless independence could be achieved, *Common Sense* also argued that America had many tactical and moral advantages that made military victory likely. America had more to fear from staying within the British Empire than from striking out on its own. Paine also looked to the future beyond independence. New state constitutions should be drafted with annually elected, single-house legislatures unfettered by governors or upper houses. The state legislatures, however, should be subservient to Congress in continental matters.

Common Sense was an immediate success. It "appeared and passed through the continent like an electric spark. It everywhere flashed conviction and aroused a determined spirit." President of Congress John Hancock wrote that the pamphlet "makes much talk here" in Philadelphia. According to Benjamin Rush, the pamphlet had "an effect which has rarely been produced by types and paper in any age or country." Delegates to Congress and others in Philadelphia sent copies to friends and family in other colonies. New Hampshire delegate Josiah Bartlett heard that the town of Portsmouth had voted against that "frightful word *Independence!*" He sent a copy of *Common Sense* as an antidote. Perhaps, he mused, "there may not appear any thing so terrible in that thought as they might at first apprehend." Abigail Adams wrote to her husband that she was "charmed with the Sentiments of *Common Sense*" and that "it is highly prized here [in Massachusetts] and carries conviction wherever it is read." Samuel Ward, delegate from Rhode Island, thought that the pamphlet should "be distributed throughout all the Colonies . . . at the public Expence." Edmund Randolph of Virginia later said that "the public sentiment which a few weeks before had shuddered at the tremendous obstacles, with which independence was environed, overleaped every barrier." Speaking of Virginia, but really describing the situation throughout America, George Washington said that "I find that '*Common Sense*' is working a powerful change there in the minds of many men."

Not everyone appreciated all of the recommendations by *Common Sense*. John Adams agreed wholeheartedly with the first part of the pamphlet advocating independence. In fact, in his autobiography written in 1802 Adams maintained that there was nothing new in the first part of the pamphlet that had not already been repeatedly advocated in Congress for nine months. But Adams thoroughly rejected Paine's plans for state and continental governments. According to Adams, Paine "has a better Hand at pulling down than building." Adams readily admitted that it would have been impossible for him to have written *Common Sense* "in so manly and striking a style," but Adams felt that he could "have made a more respectable Figure as an Architect" in creating "what is proper and necessary . . . to form Constitutions for single Colonies, as well as a great Model of Union for the whole." Not long after *Common Sense* was published, Adams published his own pamphlet, *Thoughts on Government*, which advocated a different kind of state government that was far less democratic and more balanced. Adams recollected:

Paine soon after the Appearance of my Pamphlet hurried away to my Lodgings and spent an Evening with me. His Business was to reprehend me for publishing my Pamphlet. Said he was afraid it would do hurt, and that it was repugnant to the plan he had proposed in his *Common Sense*. I told him it was true it was repugnant and for that reason, I had written it and consented to the publication of it: for I was as much afraid of his Work as he was of mine. His plan was so democratical, without any restraint or even an Attempt at any Equilibrium or Counterpoise, that it must produce confusion and every Evil Work. I told him further, that his Reasoning from the Old Testament was ridiculous, and I could hardly think him sincere. At this he laughed, and said he had taken his Ideas in that part from Milton; and then expressed a Contempt of the Old Testament and indeed of the Bible at large, which surprised me. He saw that I did not relish this, and soon checked himself, with these Words "However I have some thoughts of publishing my Thoughts on Religion, but I believe it will be best to postpone it, to the latter part of Life." This Conversation passed in good humor, without any harshness on either Side: but I perceived in him a conceit of himself, and a daring Impudence, which have been developed more and more to this day.

At least nineteen different pamphlet editions of *Common Sense* were printed in 1776 in Pennsylvania, New York, Connecticut, Rhode Island, and Massachusetts. Around 400,000 copies were sold, an amazing feat given that the entire white population numbered less than three million. Newspapers throughout the colonies reprinted excerpts from it. It can rightly be presumed that *Common Sense* was read by nearly everyone in America who could read; many others had it read to them. According to Benjamin Rush, "It was read by public men, repeated in clubs, spouted in Schools, and in one instance, delivered from the pulpit instead of a sermon by a clergyman in Connecticut." Paine had truly electrified the country; he made the people and their leaders think seriously about independence. From thinking, it is but a short step to acting. Thomas Paine had finally found his niche, as the most eloquent and persuasive spokesman of the Revolution. Throughout the remainder of the war, he wrote essays encouraging Americans to maintain their faith and to support the army and Congress however bleak the situation.

In July 1776 Paine joined the army, hoping to put his beliefs into action. Soon he became aide-de-camp to Nathanael Greene, perhaps the ablest of George Washington's generals. Paine served under Washington and Greene at the evacuations of Fort Lee and Fort Washington and the demoralizing retreat across New Jersey. He left the army in December 1776 to concentrate on writing another piece that would boost the sagging morale of the army and the country. Within days he finished the first of sixteen numbers of *The American Crisis*, which was printed in the *Pennsylvania Journal* on December 19. Four days later the essay appeared as a pamphlet and was read to Washington's troops on the banks of the Delaware as they prepared for their assault on Trenton. Even Paine's arch-enemy James Cheetham wrote in his 1809 biography that "the number was read in the camp, to every corporal's guard, and in the army and out of it had more than the intended effect." Paine's words were electrifying and inspirational:

> These are the times that try men's souls. The summer soldier and the sunshine patriot will, in this crisis, shrink from the service of their country; but he that stands it *now*, deserves the love and thanks of man and woman. Tyranny, like hell, is not easily conquered; yet we have this consolation with us, that the harder the conflict, the more glorious the triumph.

The victories that came at Trenton and Princeton were relatively unimportant militarily; in terms of morale, however, they were among the most important triumphs of the war.

The *American Crisis* solidified Paine's reputation as a man with "a capacity and a ready Pen." In January 1777 Congress appointed him secretary to a five-man delegation that met with the leadership of the Iroquois Nation seeking to keep the Indians neutral during the war. Three months later, John Adams sponsored and Congress appointed the "poor and destitute" Paine secretary to its committee for foreign affairs; but indiscretions in his public criticisms of Silas Deane and Robert Morris over their secret dealings with the French before the alliance between the two countries led to his forced resignation in January 1779. With no income, he agreed to write on behalf of the

French government for $1,000 a year, but backed out of the arrangement when offered a clerkship in a Philadelphia mercantile house. Gouverneur Morris described Paine at this time as "a mere Adventurer from England, without Fortune, without Family or Connections, ignorant even of Grammar."

In November 1779 Paine reentered government service as clerk of the Pennsylvania Assembly, and in this capacity he wrote the preamble to the Pennsylvania Emancipation Act of March 1, 1780, the first American legislation to provide for the gradual but total elimination of slavery.

The low point in the Revolution occurred in 1780. The finances of Congress were in disarray and continental currency had depreciated to worthlessness. The British shifted their operations to the South where they captured Savannah and Charleston. Mutiny threatened Washington's army, and Benedict Arnold's treason was exposed. The country's new constitution—the Articles of Confederation—submitted in November 1777 to the states for their unanimous ratification ran into an obstinate Maryland that refused to ratify until Virginia gave up its claim to its western landholdings.

Paine addressed this new crisis. In letters written in late May and early June 1780 to Blair McClenaghan, a wealthy Philadelphia merchant, and Joseph Reed, president of the Pennsylvania Supreme Executive Council, Paine called for immediate and decisive action to raise troops, money, and supplies. A draft should be implemented with bounties given to each man inducted into the army. To raise money and supplies, Paine called upon the wealthy "merchants and traders of Philadelphia to set an honorable example." Paine proposed that a subscription be raised to collect $300,000, contributed $500 himself, and pledged an additional $500. He called on the wealthy to bring in their silver plate to have it melted down and minted as coins to pay the army. "Whatever is necessary or proper to be done, must be done immediately. We must rise vigorously upon the evil, or it will rise upon us. A show of spirit will grow into real spirit." "Many a good cause has been lost or disgraced and many a man of extensive property ruined by not supporting necessary measures in time." Wealthy Philadelphians took Paine's admonishment.

They created the Bank of Pennsylvania—the first bank in America—to handle the subscribed funds for the relief of the army.

As its clerk, Paine read to the Pennsylvania Assembly a desperate letter written by General Washington on May 31, 1780, explaining the dreadful condition of the army due to lack of money and supplies. The general, in particular, criticized the congressional requisition system, in which the states were asked voluntarily to pay a stipulated share of all federal expenses. Most of the states paid only a fraction of their quotas, some paid none, and others, such as Pennsylvania, officially stated that they would not pay. According to Washington, "The crisis, in every point of view, is extraordinary." At the request of Assembly Speaker John Muhlenberg, Paine seized upon the need and paraphrased Washington's language to write *The Crisis Extraordinary*, which was published in October 1780 as a pamphlet at Paine's own expense.

Paine did not intend to map out a program for raising revenue, although he did suggest that Congress should levy a tariff. Rather, he wanted "to show the necessity and the advantages to be derived" from raising revenue by taxes and "to form the disposition of the people to the measures which I am fully persuaded it is their interest and duty to adopt, and which need no other force to accomplish them than the force of being felt." Simply put, Paine wanted to instill in people a willingness to pay taxes! He did so by arguing that it would not be difficult to raise the necessary revenue to finance the war; that British citizens were being taxed five times the amount that Americans needed to be taxed; and that the failure of Americans to support the war now would result in a British victory in which Americans would be forced to pay for the entire cost of the war through confiscation of their property and even higher taxes. Americans could win independence with moderate taxes voted by their own representatives, or they could avoid immediate taxes but suffer financial ruin under a vindictive British domination. A few days after the publication of *The Crisis Extraordinary*, Speaker Muhlenberg informed Paine "that all opposition had ceased and the house which before had been equally divided had that day been unanimous" in levying new taxes earmarked for the payment of the congressional requisition.

In late December 1780 Paine published *Public Good*, a pamphlet that systematically argued that Virginia did not legally retain the rights to land west of the Appalachian Mountains. Until Virginia ceded this land to Congress, Maryland refused to adopt the Articles of Confederation. Congress, in the meantime, operated without a written constitution, much to the dismay of Paine. *Public Good* found a receptive audience everywhere outside of Virginia. Most Virginians, including the powerful Lee family, vigorously attacked Paine as a paid lackey of the Indiana Company, which stood to profit from a Virginia cession. But even Virginia appreciated Paine's logic, and the Old Dominion ceded its western holdings to Congress in 1781.

Throughout the war, Paine aligned himself in Pennsylvania with the radical Constitutionalist Party that vigorously supported the democratic state Constitution of 1776. He differed with Constitutionalists, however, in supporting increased powers for Congress. At the end of *Public Good*, Paine called for a national convention to draft a new federal constitution. The Articles of Confederation, still unadopted, had too many flaws, and the powers of Congress "appeared to be too much in some cases and too little in others." Properly enumerated federal powers would "give additional energy to the whole, and a new confidence to the several parts."

Throughout most of 1780 Paine formulated a bizarre scheme in which he planned to sneak back into England and support the American cause through various publications. Success in America had gone to his head, and he believed that he could change the disposition of any people through his writing. Paine first told General Nathanael Greene about the plan and the general told his friend "to defer the matter." Later Paine proposed the plan to Pennsylvania President Joseph Reed, who felt that the project was "both difficult and dangerous." Under the guise of needing time to collect and organize material for a history of the Revolution, Paine asked the Pennsylvania Assembly for a year's leave of absence. When the Assembly refused, Paine resigned and booked passage for England. Again, General Greene intervened with a forceful letter "strongly dissuading" Paine from undertaking the foolhardy venture. The execution of British spy Major John André for his role in Benedict Arnold's treason convinced Paine that he might become "an object of retaliation" should he be captured in England. He gave up the gambit.

Despite the success of *The Crisis Extraordinary*, it became obvious that America needed increased French assistance. Paine proposed that Congress ask French Foreign Minister Vergennes for a loan or subsidy of £1 million a year for the duration of the war and he drafted a letter to this effect. Congress endorsed the idea and appointed John Laurens as emissary to explain the request at the French court. Laurens asked Paine to accompany him as secretary, but opposition in Congress quashed Paine's appointment. He nonetheless joined Laurens as an unofficial adviser. They left Philadelphia in mid-January 1781 for Boston and left Boston a month later aboard the Continental frigate *Alliance*. After a quick but dangerous voyage of twenty-three days, battling icebergs and British privateers, the Americans arrived safely in France on March 9. After ten weeks of negotiations, in which Benjamin Franklin played a crucial role, the French agreed to gifts and loans worth 25 million livres. Laurens, Paine, and much of the French aid arrived in Boston on August 25. Laurens rushed off to join Washington's army as it marched toward Yorktown, while Paine escorted the wagonloads of French assistance to Philadelphia. Late in life, Paine would argue that the French gold he and Laurens brought to America kept the army in the field and enabled the victory won at Yorktown.

While in France, Paine had attracted attention as the author of *Common Sense*. His renown did not obscure his personal peculiarities to those who knew him. Elkanah Watson, the future canal builder, described the unkempt appearance of his fellow boardinghouse resident.

> He was coarse and uncouth in his manners, loathsome in his appearance, and a disgusting egotist; rejoicing most in talking of himself, and reading the effusions of his own mind. Yet I could not repress the deepest emotions of gratitude towards him, as the instrument of Providence in accelerating the declaration of our Independence. . . .
>
> On his arrival being announced, the Mayor, and some of the most distinguished citizens of Nantes, called upon him to render their homage of respect. I often officiated as interpreter,

although humbled and mortified at his filthy appearance, and awkward and unseemly address. Besides, as he had been roasted alive on his arrival at L'Orient, for the * * * * and well basted with brimstone, he was absolutely offensive, and perfumed the whole apartment. He was soon rid of his respectable visitors, who left the room with marks of astonishment and disgust. I took the liberty, on his asking for the loan of a clean shirt, of speaking to him frankly of his dirty appearance and brimstone odor, and prevailed upon him to stew for an hour, in a hot bath. This, however, was not done without much entreaty, and I did not succeed, until receiving a file of English newspapers, I promised, after he was in the bath, he should have the reading of them, and not before. He at once consented, and accompanied me to the bath, where I instructed the keeper in French (which Paine did not understand) to gradually increase the heat of the water, until "le Monsieur était bien bouilli." He became so much absorbed in his reading that he was nearly par-boiled before leaving the bath, much to his improvement and my satisfaction.

With the American victory at Yorktown in October 1781, the war went into hibernation for the winter. On January 24, 1782, a deputation of army officers approached Paine to ask him to write a petition to General Washington requesting the officers' back pay. Paine remembered what happened when he wrote a similar petition nine years earlier to increase the salaries of excise tax collectors in England—he was fired. This time Paine declined to write the petition because the Treasury was unable to pay immediately and that such a petition would add "to the distress of the General." Paine asked the officers to be patient, "mentioning that the State of the Treasury was now improving, that the Taxes laid this year were real and valuable and that any pressing demands just now might rather injure than promote their interest." Paine wrote to Superintendent of Finance Robert Morris to suggest that the officers might be satisfied with interest payments on their back pay; Morris worked out a temporary plan for the officers.

Washington and Morris realized that Paine's services might still be valuable. Despondent and impoverished, Paine sought public employment, but Congress rebuffed him. Washington asked Paine to be patient and twice approached Superintendent Morris to seek a position for Paine. Morris concocted a scheme that called for paying Paine $800 a year, paid quarterly, to write "in support of the measures of Congress and their Ministers." Washington "agreed entirely in the plan," and Secretary for Foreign Affairs Robert R. Livingston also endorsed the measure. In an official memorandum of agreement, Morris, Livingston, and Washington acknowledged "the important Situation of Affairs in the present moment, and the Propriety and even necessity of informing the People and rousing them into Action." Morris later outlined Paine's duties.

Having these for our objects we want the aid of an able pen to urge the Legislatures of the several States to grant sufficient taxes; to grant those taxes separate and distinct from those levied for State purposes; to put such taxes, or rather the money arising from them, in the power of Congress, from the moment of collection;

To grant permanent revenues for discharging the interest on debts already contracted, or that may be contracted;

To extend by a new confederation the powers of Congress, so that they may be competent to the government of the United States and the management of their affairs;

To prepare the minds of the people for such restraints and such taxes and imposts, as are absolutely necessary for their own welfare;

To comment from time to time on military transactions, so as to place in a proper point of view the bravery, good conduct, and soldiership of our officers and troops, when they deserve applause and to do the same on such conduct of such civil officers or citizens, as act conspicuously for the service of their country.

Livingston, who would supply Paine with confidential "intelligence, as might be necessary from time to time," would employ Paine in his department using secret-service funds supplied by Morris. No one but the four men (and Gouverneur Morris, Robert Morris's assistant) was to know of the covert appointment "lest the publications might lose their force if it were known that the author is paid for them by government" and so that Paine would not be subject "to injurious personal Reflections."

Paine accepted the appointment without hesitation, believing that it was offered "not only out of friendship to me, but out of justice." He also knew that he could still serve the Revolutionary cause, but not without a source of income. Feeling a sense of pride in the appointment, Paine probably divulged the secret to his friend President Joseph Reed, who told Nathanael Greene that Paine was "a hireling writer pensioned with £300 per annum, payable by General Washington out of the secret service money." For the next two years Paine wrote in support of Superintendent Morris's attempts to raise revenue and increase the powers of Congress.

Late in the war, the Marquis de Chastellux and Lafayette joined John Laurens to meet with Paine at the latter's quarters. Chastellux

> discovered, at his apartments, all the attributes of a man of letters; a room pretty much in disorder, dusty furniture, and a large table covered with books lying open, and manuscripts begun. His person was in a correspondent dress, nor did his physiognomy belie the spirit that reigns throughout his works. Our conversation was agreeable and animated. . . . His existence at Philadelphia is similar to that of those political writers in England, who have obtained nothing, and have neither credit enough in the state, nor sufficient political weight to obtain a part in the affairs of government. Their works are read with more curiosity than confidence, their projects being regarded rather as the play of imagination, than as well concerted plans, and sufficient in credit ever to produce any real effect: theirs is always considered as the work of an individual, and not that of a party; information may be drawn from them, but not consequences; accordingly we observe, that the influence of these authors is more felt in the satirical, than in the dogmatical style, as it is easier for them to decry other men's opinions than to establish their own. This is more the case with Mr. Payne than any body; for having formerly held a post in government, he has now no connection with it; and as his patriotism and his talents are unquestionable, it is natural to conclude that the vivacity of his imagination, and the independence of his charac-

ter, render him more calculated for reasoning on affairs, than for conducting them.

Sarah Bache wrote to her father, Benjamin Franklin, in France that Paine had alienated most people in Philadelphia.

There never was a man less beloved in a place than Payne is in this, having at different times disputed with everybody. The most rational thing he could have done would have been to have died the instant he had finished his *Common Sense*, for he never again will have it in his power to leave the World with so much credit.

On March 23, 1783, word arrived from France that a preliminary peace treaty had been signed. With peace imminent, Paine readied his last *Crisis* essay, which was published on April 19, 1783, the eighth anniversary of the battles of Lexington and Concord. The essay began: "'The times that tried men's souls,' are over—and the greatest and compleatest revolution the world ever knew is gloriously and happily accomplished." Paine wrote,

Independence always appeared to me practicable and probable; provided the sentiment of the country could be formed and held to the object: and there is no instance in the world, where a people so extended, and wedded to former habits of thinking, and under such a variety of circumstances, were so instantly and effectually pervaded, by a turn in politics, as in the case of independence, and who supported their opinion, undiminished, through such a succession of good and ill fortune, till they crowned it with success.

More than any other person, Thomas Paine was responsible for changing those "former habits of thinking" in abandoning the British Empire and rejecting monarchism for republicanism. Paine did more than anyone else except Washington to sustain the morale of the American people through "good and ill fortune."

Now that the military victory and independence had been achieved, Paine had other great purposes for America to pursue. It was now "in our power to make a world happy—to teach mankind the art of being so—to exhibit on the theater of the universe a character hitherto unknown—and to have, as it were, a new creation entrusted to our hands." America should let "the world see that she can bear prosperity; and that her honest virtue in time of peace, is equal to the bravest virtue in time of war." Americans should never forget "that a fair national reputation is of as much importance as independence. That it possesses a charm which wins upon the world, and makes even enemies civil. That it gives dignity which is often superior to power, and commands reverence where pomp and splendor fail." To maintain its position in the world, Americans were exhorted to maintain and strengthen the Union of the states. "As UNITED STATES we are equal to the importance of the title, but otherwise we are not."

Paine repeated this argument in December 1783 in an essay attacking Britain's discriminatory commercial policies toward America. America must expect this kind of treatment from other countries "unless she guards her Union with nicer care and stricter honor. United, she is formidable. . . . Separated, she is a medley of individual nothings, subject to the sport of foreign Nations." It was "only by acting in Union" that the usurpation of foreign countries in trade could be counteracted. "When we view a Flag, which to the eye is beautiful, and to contemplate its rise and origin, inspires a sensation of sublime delight, our National Honor must unite with our Interest to prevent injury to the one, or insult to the other."

Victory vindicated the author of *Common Sense*, but it also took away his raison d'être. Paine was a political writer and nothing else. What would he do now? Robert Morris had resigned as superintendent of finance and his position had been replaced by a three-man Board of Treasury—one of whom, Arthur Lee, had been Paine's enemy ever since his *Public Good* essay argued against Virginia's claims to western lands. Paine hinted that Congress ought to give him a pension. In the last number of *The Crisis*, he wrote that "From me the states have received the unremitted service of seven years, and to them I have not been the expense of a private soldier. I have done every thing *of* myself and *from* myself. The interest of the heart alone has carried me through a thousand things which others would have failed in or staggered at. . . . I never sought," he wrote, "place, office, nor reward, since I have been in America." But he could not "help viewing my situation as singularly inconvenient. Trade I do not understand. Land I have none, or what is equal to none. I have exiled myself from one Country without making a home of another; and I cannot help sometimes asking myself, what am I better off than a refugee?" But Congress did not offer a pension. Instead it considered naming Paine its official historian with an annual salary to write a history of the Revolution. Paine liked the title but wanted to be compensated for past services; he did not wish an annual income for future service that would depend on the vagaries of congressional politics. Furthermore, he believed that his history would be viewed as tainted if Congress subsidized him. Congress took no action, but French Minister Luzerne presented Paine with a gift of 2,300 livres for past services with which Paine bought a small farm near Bordentown, New Jersey.

Paine complained to a number of friends about Congress's coolness. He told Washington that

> I am hurt by the neglect of the collective ostensible body of America, in a way which it is probable they do not perceive my feelings. It has an effect in putting either my reputation or their generosity at stake; for it cannot fail of suggesting that either I (notwithstanding the appearance of service) have been undeserving their regard or that they are remiss towards me. Their silence is to me something like condemnation, and their neglect must be justified by my loss of reputation, or my reputation supported at their injury; either of which is alike painful to me. But as I have ever been dumb on everything which might touch national honor so I mean ever to continue so.

Paine asked other friends for assistance in securing gifts or pensions from state legislatures. In December 1783 he wrote to New York City Mayor James Duane complaining, "I am tired of having no home, especially in a country where, everybody will allow, I have deserved one." If Congress and the states gave him no relief, Paine told Duane he would be forced to go to Europe. He asked Duane to lobby for a small piece of land expropriated by the state from Loyalists. Duane and Lewis Morris worked with the state senate, which unanimously resolved to offer Paine one of two properties "for the eminent Services rendered to the United States in the Progress of the late War . . . and as a Testimony of the Sense which the People of this State entertain of his distinguished Merit." In spring of 1784, Paine selected a 300-acre farm in New Rochelle about thirty miles northeast of New York City worth at least £1,000. In a small ceremony officially turning the property over, the legislature's ode to Paine was read. "His literary works . . . inspired the citizens of this state with unanimity, confirmed their confidence in the rectitude of their cause, and have ultimately contributed to the freedom, sovereignty and independence of the United States." Because of the remoteness of the farm, however, Paine did not choose to reside on it, but arranged to have Lewis Morris manage it.

George Washington wrote to James Madison, Patrick Henry, and Richard Henry Lee seeking assistance from Virginia for Paine. "His writings certainly have had a powerful effect on the public mind; ought they not then to meet an adequate return?" Thomas Jefferson thought Virginia should give him £2,000 or property that would draw an annual income of £100. Madison promoted such a bill in the Virginia House of Delegates but it was defeated by one vote when Arthur Lee reminded the delegates that Paine had written against Virginia's western landholdings. A disappointed Jefferson still hoped that something could be done for Paine. "He richly deserves it; and it will give a character of littleness to our state if they suffer themselves to be restrained from the compensation due for his services by the paltry consideration that he opposed our right to the Western country. Who was there out of Virginia who did not oppose it?"

In April 1785 the Pennsylvania Assembly awarded Paine £500 as a "temporary compensation" for his services. Another grant was expected if Congress failed to offer Paine assistance. Congress, however, reconsidered Paine's request during the summer of 1785. On August 26, it resolved that "Mr. Paine is entitled to a liberal gratification from the United States." In September Congress defeated a motion by Elbridge Gerry to provide Paine a gift of $6,000; on October 3 it approved a $3,000 gift. No state favored Paine after this action by Congress.

Paine avoided political controversy while his financial appeals were pending before Congress and the state legislatures. He went into semiretirement, spending most of his time in Bordentown, New Jersey, where he developed plans and a model of an iron bridge that he hoped to construct in Philadelphia across the Schuykill River. But as soon as Congress made its grant, Paine jumped back into the political fray. When his old friends in the Pennsylvania Assembly issued paper money on loan to landowners and revoked the charter of the Bank of North America, Paine criticized these acts in a pamphlet entitled *Dissertations on Government; the Affairs of the Bank; and Paper Money*. Repeatedly his former allies attacked Paine as "an unprincipled author whose pen is let out for hire," "who, having reaped a recompense more than adequate to his deserts, prostitutes his pen to the ruin of his country." Paine defended his stance, arguing that he had supported the bank from its inception in 1780 as the Bank of Pennsylvania and that he had consistently opposed paper money since the collapse of the continental currency. He made the distinction between ordinary laws that were reversible by the legislature and contractual laws such as the bank's charter that could only be repealed if acceptable to both parties. The U.S. Supreme Court under John Marshall would use Paine's reasoning thirty-three years later in the Dartmouth College case.

In late September 1786 Paine further alienated his former allies. In a newspaper article entitled "On the Affairs of State," he argued against Pennsylvania's single-house legislature. He had supported unicameralism in *Common Sense* in 1776 and two years later when opponents mounted an effort to alter Pennsylvania's constitution. Eight years later, however, Paine's attitude had changed. "My aim [in 1778] was to quiet the dispute, and prevent it from entangling the country, at a time when the utmost harmony of its powers was necessary to its safety. The constitution was upon experiment, and the manner in which a single house would use an abundance of power would best determine whether it ought to be trusted with it." He hoped that the will of the people would be responsibly represented in the single-house assembly. Unfortunately, human nature operated in a single body as it does in a single individual. Executives were thought to be the dangerous element in government in 1776; experience had shown that tyranny could also emanate from a legislative body.

Paine also felt that the federal constitution—the Articles of Confederation—had not lived up to expectations. He had always wanted a strengthened central government to which the states would be subordinate on national matters. In 1784 and 1785 he proposed a stronger national government. By the end of 1786 many Americans came to share Paine's opinion. A constitutional convention was called to meet in Philadelphia in May 1787 to revise the Articles. Paine, however, would not be able to participate in the convention or in the vehement public debate that followed. On April 26, 1787, he left America for France and England to visit his parents and to win endorsements of his iron bridge from prominent scientists. Expecting to return before winter, he was gone for fifteen years.

Paine greatly enjoyed his first two years in Europe as he traveled back and forth between France and England. He arrived in France on May 26, 1787, after an uneventful ocean crossing. Letters of introduction from Franklin opened many doors, and Paine enjoyed the gracious hospitality of Jefferson, now in Paris as U.S. minister to France. After three months, Paine left France with the endorsement of the French Academy of Sciences for his bridge. He traveled to London seeking the Royal Society's endorsement.

Early in his visit to England, Paine visited Thetford. His father had died the previous year, but his ninety-one-year-old mother still lived. Paine settled a pension on her. Most of his time was spent in London, where he met and became friendly with Edmund Burke. After three months in England he returned to France without a decision from the Royal Society about his bridge. He arrived back in France in December 1787 for a short stay before returning to England, where he received a patent for his bridge. By late April 1789 a scaled-down version of the bridge had been constructed and a full-sized version was begun. During this time, Jefferson kept Paine informed of the political events occurring in France. On July 14, 1789, the Bastille was stormed. Sensing revolution in the air, Paine longed to travel back to France. "A share in two revolutions is living to some purpose." But in October 1789 Paine's business partner in the bridge construction was thrown into debtors prison for bankruptcy. Because Paine's name had been used on £620 worth of debt, he too was held in debtors prison for three weeks while awaiting funds from America. Immediately upon his release, he left for Paris, where the revolutionary fervor mounted.

In February 1790, a frightened Edmund Burke delivered his first assault in Parliament against the French Revolution. His speech was published and a longer pamphlet by Burke attacking the revolution was anticipated. A month later, Paine returned to England to combat Burke. Before leaving, Lafayette gave Paine the key to the Bastille to present to Washington. Unwilling to abandon his second revolution, Paine forwarded the key to Washington with a note saying that

> I feel myself happy in being the person through whom the Marquis has conveyed this early trophy of the spoils of despotism, and the first ripe fruits of American principles transplanted into Europe, to his master and patron. When he mentioned to me the present he intended you, my heart leaped with joy. It is something so truly in character, that no remarks can illustrate it, and is more happily expressive of his remembrance of his American friends, than any letters can convey. That the principles of America opened the Bastille is not to be doubted; and therefore the key comes to the right place.

On November 1, 1790, Burke published his *Reflections on the Revolution in France*, which immediately became an enormous success. Friends of the Revolution residing in England published over seventy defenses of the French occurrences. In mid-March 1791 Paine, then in London, published the first part of his *Rights of Man*, which outlined the principles of the revolutions of 1776 and 1789. Government existed solely to defend those natural rights—life, liberty, property, security, and resistance to oppression—which man was incapable of protecting himself. After securing these rights, the best government did as little as possible. A republican form of government best secured these rights. Every government should be limited by a bill of rights and a written constitution, which should include universal manhood suffrage, regular and frequent elections of the legislature and executive officers (with the latter subject to a mandatory rotation in office), a judiciary subject to some control by the people, and a prohibition of titles of nobility.

Paine published the second part of *Rights of Man* in February 1792 and meant it to be the British equivalent of *Common Sense*. It called for the overthrow of the monarchy and the establishment of a republic. By 1793 over 200,000 copies were sold despite the efforts of the British government to suppress it. The author, who by now had fled to France, was tried for treason, convicted, and outlawed in December 1792. Gouverneur Morris, serving as special envoy to Great Britain, described Paine as having "an excellent Pen to write . . . but an indifferent Head to think." William Short, America's chargé d'affaires in France noted the shortcomings in Paine's style but praised his "strong expressions and bold ideas." The Frenchman Etienne Dumont captured the dichotomy that was Paine.

> I could easily excuse, in an American, his prejudice against England but his egregious conceit and presumptuous self-sufficiency quite disgusted me. He was drunk with vanity. If you believed him, it was he who had done everything in America. He was an absolute caricature of the vainest of Frenchmen. He fancied that his book upon the Rights of Man ought to be substituted for every other book in the world; and he told us roundly that, if it were in his power to annihilate every library in existence, he would do so without hesitation in order to eradicate the errors they contained and commence with the Rights of Man, a new era of ideas and principles. He knew all his own writings by heart, but he knew nothing else. . . . Yet Paine was a man of talent, full of imagination, gifted with popular eloquence, and wielded, not without skill, the weapon of irony.

In August 1792, the French National Convention made Paine, Washington, Alexander Hamilton, James Madison, and a number of prominent Europeans French citizens. The following month Paine was elected by four different departments to sit in the National Convention. (He chose to represent Pas de Calais.) He aligned with the moderate, well-to-do Girondin coalition, but broke ranks when he spoke against the execution of Louis XVI, advocating imprisonment during the war and thereafter permanent exile to America. When the Girondins fell from power, Paine went into semiretirement. The Jacobins, however, revoked his French citizenship and his parliamentary immunity, and, on December 28, 1793, incarcerated him in the Luxembourg Prison in Paris as a citizen of a country at war with France.

Imprisoned by France and outlawed by England, Paine was abandoned by the United States. President Washington, under heavy pressure from Federalists sympathetic to England and Jeffersonian Republicans supportive of France, was intent on maintaining the neutrality of the United States. His administration held that Paine had renounced his American citizenship when he accepted French citizenship and agreed to serve in the French National Convention. America thus had no grounds to intervene on his behalf; and, even if he were an American citizen, he would still be personally responsible for violations of French law while resident in France. U.S. Minister to France Gouverneur Morris, never a friend of Paine's, told Washington that Paine was actually safer in the obscurity of prison than free facing the bloodthirsty justice of the revolutionary courts. Feeling betrayed by Washington, Paine became embittered. His hopes were buoyed, however, when James Monroe replaced Morris as American minister. Given no formal instructions concerning Paine, Monroe worked privately for two months before obtaining Paine's release in November 1794.

Weakened and impoverished by his ordeal, Paine accepted Monroe's invitation to live with him. The demanding and sometimes obnoxious guest stayed a year and a half, during which time the National Convention restored him to his seat. Paine addressed the convention and reiterated his faith in the Revolution. Paine, however, had lost faith in Washington and in 1796 published a bitter denunciation of the president for his treachery. "He has acted towards me the part of a cold blooded traitor."

While imprisoned, Paine worked on the *Age of Reason* (Part I) in which he denounced the trappings of formal Christianity. Paine avowed a belief "in one God, and no more" and the possibility of "happiness beyond this life." The existence of God, in Paine's judgment, was discernible only through reason.

The only idea man can affix to the name of God, is, that of a *first cause*, the cause of all things. And incomprehensibly difficult as it

27

is for man to conceive what a first cause is, he arrives at the belief of it, from the tenfold greater difficulty of disbelieving it. It is difficult beyond description to conceive that space can have no end; but it is more difficult to conceive an end. It is difficult beyond the power of man to conceive an eternal duration of what we call time; but it is more impossible to conceive a time when there shall be no time. In like manner of reasoning, every thing we behold carries in itself the internal evidence that it did not make itself . . . ; and it is the conviction arising from this evidence, that carries us on, as it were, by necessity, to the belief of a first cause eternally existing, of a nature totally different to any material existence we know of, and by the power of which all things exist, and this first cause man calls God.

The word of God was not to be found in the Bible, or in any human language. It is revealed in the creation of the universe visible every day in nature. "All other bibles and testaments are to him forgeries." In the second part of the *Age of Reason*, published in 1795, Paine systematically analyzed the Bible and, in his judgment, proved it unworthy to be the word of God. The *Rights of Man* subverted belief in the traditional form of government people were accustomed to; the *Age of Reason* did the same with traditional Christianity and the Bible. Paine's old friend, Benjamin Rush, said that the *Age of Reason* "demoralized half the Christian world." According to Rush, this book "probably perverted more persons from the Christian faith than any book that ever was written for the same purpose. Its extensive mischief was owing to the popular, perspicuous, and witty style in which it was written, and to its constant appeals to the feelings and tempers of his readers."

When peace temporarily returned in Europe in 1802, Paine seized the opportunity for a safe passage back to the United States. On October 30 his ship docked in Baltimore. It was not the same Tom Paine who had left America fifteen years earlier. According to Tennessee Congressman William Dickson, the "energy of mind and forcible language of which he was formerly possessed is gone. He is now in the sixty-sixth year of his age, but the hardships sustained in the French Prisons have made him much older—he receives due attention from the Republicans." In November 1802 while visiting in

Washington, D.C., Eli Whitney, the inventor of the cotton gin and interchangeable parts for muskets, heard that Paine was in town. The Connecticut inventor "had some curiosity to see him" and was surprised to find that Paine and he resided in the same public boarding house. When Whitney went to dinner he sat immediately across the table from Paine and "was not disappointed in my expectation of his appearance—I found him the same filthy old sot that he has ever been represented." From his appearance, Whitney judged that Paine was nearly seventy years old.

> He is about five feet 10 inches high—his hair three-fourth white—black eyes—a large bulbous nose—a large mouth drawn down at the corners with flabby lips—with more than half decayed, horrid looking teeth—his complexion of a brick color—his face & nose covered with carbuncles & spots of a darker hue than the general color of his skin—his dress rather mean & his whole appearance very slovenly—his hands so convulsed that while his expansive lips almost encompassed a wine glass, he could hardly get the contents of it into his head without spilling it. . . . In short he is a mere loathsome carcass, which has withstood the ravages & rackings of brutal intemperance for an uncommon length of time & from which (were it exposed on the barren heath of Africa) the Hyena & Jackals would turn away with disgust.

While in Washington, President Jefferson cordially welcomed him into his home. According to Jefferson, Mr. Paine "is too well entitled to the hospitality of every American not to cheerfully receive mine." Whitney reported that Paine was a "bosome friend" of the president. "Though some of the democrats will swallow common carrion with a good relish, I think most of them will loath the putrid rattle snake which has died from the venom of his own bite."

Immediately and repeatedly Federalists condemned Paine as an atheistic blasphemer. Paine could not resist the urge to retaliate against his Federalist critics. In four letters addressed to the citizens of the United States, he denounced his enemies, describing their scurrilous assaults as the "little barkings of scribblings and witless curs who pass for nothing." Paine, however, saw that the vehemence directed at him personally might have a deleterious effect on the Jeffersonians in the next election—perhaps even resulting in the defeat of President Jefferson. Consequently, Paine tried to defuse some of the hatred that had been generated by his public criticism of President Washington and by his assault on the Bible and Christianity in the *Age of Reason*. In December 1802, Paine's old and deeply religious friend Samuel Adams, now eighty years old, asked Paine about his motivation in writing "a defense of infidelity." Paine's response to Adams, dated January 1, 1803, was widely printed in newspapers. He wrote that

> Every man's creed who has any creed at all, is *I believe in God*. . . . Do we want to contemplate His power? We see it in the immensity of the Creation. Do we want to contemplate His wisdom? We see it in the unchangeable order by which the incomprehensible WHOLE is governed. Do we want to contemplate His munificence? We see it in the abundance with which He fills the earth. Do we want to contemplate His mercy? We see it in His not withholding that abundance even from the unthankful. In fine, do we want to know what GOD is? Search not written or printed books, but the Scripture called the *creation*.

Paine told Adams that

> A man does not serve God when he prays, for it is himself he is trying to serve . . . but instead of buffeting the Deity with prayers as if I distrusted Him, or must dictate to Him, I reposed myself on His protection; and you, my friend, will find, even in your last moments, more consolation in the silence of resignation than in the murmuring wish of a prayer. The key of heaven is not in the keeping of any sect, nor ought the road to it be obstructed by any. Our relation to each other in this World is as men, and the man who is a friend to man and to his rights, let his religious opinions be what they may, is a good citizen.

Paine yearned for tolerance of man for man. "Between Men in pursuit of truth, and whose object is the happiness of Man both here and hereafter, there ought to be no reserve. Even Error has a claim to indulgence, if not to respect, when it is believed to be truth."

Paine left Washington in mid-February 1803. On his way to New York, he stopped in Philadelphia to renew old friendships. Some men such as Charles Willson Peale greeted him warmly; others such as Benjamin Rush ostracized him. Wherever he went someone always sneered behind his back or refused to offer him some kind of service. To many people, Paine was the devil incarnate. In New York City, however, he was welcomed as a hero. The many recent immigrants from Great Britain had read the *Rights of Man* and agreed with Paine's castigation of the British government.

During his last years, Paine occasionally advised President Jefferson. Whenever Jefferson wrestled with a particularly thorny problem, he would ask Paine for an opinion. Such was the case over the Louisiana Purchase. In December 1802, Paine advised Jefferson to buy the entire Louisiana Territory from France, not merely the island upon which New Orleans was situated. A subtle hint to France that Americans in the western territory would soon seize Louisiana coupled with France's desperate financial condition made such a purchase likely. When the opportunity to purchase the whole Louisiana Territory presented itself, Jefferson struggled with the constitutionality of such an act. Paine advised that "The cession makes no alteration in the Constitution; it only extends the principles of it over a larger territory, and this certainly is within the morality of the Constitution, and not contrary to, nor beyond, the expression of intention of any of its articles." Paine later advised the president not to allow the French and Spanish residents of Louisiana to keep their legal system and French as their official language. Louisiana should be brought into the American Union completely, lest the demand for separation and independence arise. Paine advised the president to assist in settling free blacks in the new territory. Congress should provide for their transportation west. Free blacks should upon arrival contract themselves out to planters for a year or two and then purchase their own land. An even better plan, Paine suggested, would be to encourage Europeans to immigrate to the territory. German redemptioners—like those who had immigrated to Pennsylvania—were the best prospects. They were hard workers and Protestants, and thus would neutralize the predominant Catholic population.

With Jefferson reelected president in 1804 and Federalists soundly defeated throughout the country, Paine decided "I shall do as I did after the war, remain a quiet spectator and attend now to my own affairs." He still, however, wrote occasional pieces in which he attacked Federalists, condemned corrupt New York politicians, explained the cause of yellow fever, and advocated a gunboat defense for America's coastline. But a lonely life with occasional periods of drunkenness and financial difficulty plagued him. In the spring of 1806, a friend rescued him from a drunken stupor that had lasted for more than two weeks. The friend cleaned him up and brought him to his home in New York City where Paine lived for several months. Somewhat senile, Paine moved out, dissatisfied with and ungrateful for the attention given him. His final years were spent in and around New York City. Old friends occasionally came by his residence to pay their respects. Sometimes Paine was pleased to see them and they would share memories; other times he would reject those who had ignored him for years. When visited by Albert Gallatin and his wife, Paine told them, "I am very sorry that I ever returned to this country." He died on June 8, 1809. In his will, written five months before his death, Paine reflected that "I have lived an honest and useful life to mankind; my time has been spent in doing good, and I die in perfect composure and resignation to the will of my Creator, God."

In a variation of the biographer's eternal question, Thomas Paine once said that "he was at a loss to know whether he was made for the times or the times made for him." In the last number of *The Crisis*, he wrote that "It was the cause of America that made me an author." There is no doubt that Paine fit and shaped his times. His talent for writing was remarkable. Benjamin Rush wrote that "He possessed a wonderful talent of writing to the tempers and feelings of the public." Discarding the ornamentation and stylistic rules of his era, he wrote in a simple, direct prose readily understood by everyone. Through the use of provocative assertions and vivid original imagery, his writings were always geared to and understood by the common people. In answering one of his critics during the winter of 1778-1779, he announced his "design to make those that can scarcely read understand." In the first *American Crisis* essay he vowed not to dwell "upon the vapors of imagination; I bring reason to your ears; and in language as plain as A, B, C, hold up truth to your eyes." It was the cause of America, he said, that "made it impossible for me, feeling as I did, to be silent." During the revolutionary years, he rendered invaluable services to his adopted country, while he "likewise added something to the reputation of literature, by freely and disinterestedly employing it in the great cause of mankind, and showing there may be genius without prostitution." He would always be proud of his role and be grateful "to Nature and Providence for putting it in my power to be of some use to mankind." In a letter to Henry Laurens, Paine admitted that he was "neither farmer, manufacturer, mechanic, merchant nor shopkeeper. . . . I am," he said, "a *Farmer of thoughts.*" Throughout his life he sowed the seeds of ideas. No "summer soldier or sunshine patriot," Paine remained committed to stating the truth as he saw it, despite the consequences. His vision of a humane and democratic society shaped a philosophy for his time. That philosophy still speaks to us today.

THE WORDS OF
PAINE

Action

Whatever is necessary or proper to be done, must be done immediately. We must rise vigorously upon the evil, or it will rise upon us. A show of spirit will grow into real spirit.

To Joseph Reed, June 4, 1780

Adaptability

It is the faculty of the human mind to become what it contemplates, and to act in unison with its object.

Rights of Man, I, 1791

There is a natural aptness in man, and more so in society, because it embraces a greater variety of abilities and resource, to accommodate itself to whatever situation it is in.

Rights of Man, II, 1792

Adversity

I love the man that can smile in trouble, that can gather strength from distress, and grow brave by reflection. 'Tis the business of little minds to shrink; but he whose heart is firm, and whose conscience approves his conduct, will pursue his principles unto death.

The American Crisis, 1776

Advice

❦

That advice should be taken where example has failed, or precept be regarded where warning is ridiculed, is like a picture of hope resting on despair.

The Crisis, 1780

Aesop's Fables

❦

With respect to Aesop, though the moral is in general just, the fable is often cruel; and the cruelty of the fable does more injury to the heart, especially in a child, than the moral does good to the judgment.

Age of Reason, II, 1795

Agriculture

❦

Cultivation is, at least, one of the greatest natural improvements ever made by human invention. It has given to created earth a ten-fold value.

Agrarian Justice, 1797

Alarms

❧ ❧

It is always dangerous to spread an alarm of danger unless the prospect of success be held out with it, and that not only as probable, but naturally essential.

To Joseph Reed, June 4, 1780

Altering Government

❧ ❧

The right of altering the government was a natural right, and not a right of government.

Rights of Man, I, 1791

Ambition

❧ ❧

I am not an ambitious man, but perhaps I have been an ambitious American. I have wished to see America the *Mother Church* of government.

To James Monroe, September 10, 1794

Amendments

❧ ❧

It will always happen, when a thing is originally wrong, that amendments do not make it right.

Rights of Man, I, 1791

America

❧ ❦

This Continent is too extensive to sleep all at once, and too watchful, even in its slumbers, not to startle at the unhallowed foot of an invader.

The American Crisis, 1777

America is her own mistress and can do what she pleases.

The American Crisis, 1778

America ever is what she thinks herself to be.

The Crisis, 1780

Government and the people do not in America constitute distinct bodies. They are one, and their interest the same. Members of Congress, members of Assembly, or Council, or by any other name they may be called, are only a selected part of the people. They are the representatives of majesty, but not majesty itself. The dignity exists inherently in the universal multitude, and though it may be delegated, cannot be alienated.

The Necessity of Taxation, 1782

America is a new character in the universe. She started with a cause divinely right, and struck at an object vast and valuable. Her reputation for political integrity, perseverance, fortitude, and all the manly excellencies, stands high in the world.

The Necessity of Taxation, 1782

America as a Religious Asylum

❧ ❦

The time . . . at which the continent was discovered, adds weight to the argument [for independence from Great Britain], and the manner in which it was peopled increases the force of it. The reformation was preceded by the discovery of America, as if the Almighty graciously meant to open a sanctuary to the persecuted in future years, when home should afford neither friendship nor safety.

Common Sense, 1776

America as an Example of Freedom

❧ ❧

The cause of America is, in a great measure, the cause of all mankind.

Common Sense, 1776

We have it in our power to begin the world over again. A situation, similar to the present, hath not happened since the days of Noah until now. The birthday of a new world is at hand, and a race of men, perhaps as numerous as all Europe contains, are to receive their portion of freedom from the event of a few months. The Reflection is awful.

Common Sense, 1776

Could the mist of antiquity be taken away, and men and things viewed as they then really were, it is more than probable that they [the ancient Greeks and Romans] would admire us, rather than we them. America has surmounted a greater variety and combination of difficulties than, I believe, ever fell to the share of any one people, in the same space of time, and has replenished the world with more useful knowledge and sounder maxims of civil government than were ever produced in any age before. Had it not been for America there had been no such thing as freedom left throughout the whole universe.

The American Crisis, 1778

To see it in our power to make a world happy—to teach mankind the art of being so—to exhibit on the theater of the universe a character hitherto unknown—and to have, as it were, a new creation entrusted to our hands, are honors that command reflection, and can neither be too highly estimated, nor too gratefully received.

The Crisis, 1783

America needs never be ashamed to tell her birth, nor relate the stages by which she rose to empire.

The Crisis, 1783

Our very good friend, the Marquis de Lafayette, has entrusted to my care the key of the Bastille, and a drawing handsomely framed, representing the demolition of that detestable prison, as a present to your Excellency, of which his letter will more particularly inform. I feel myself happy in being the person through whom the Marquis has conveyed this early trophy of the spoils of despotism, and the first ripe fruits of American principles transplanted into Europe, to his master and patron. When he mentioned to me the present he intended you, my heart, leaped with joy. It is something so truly in character, that no remarks can illustrate it, and is more happily expressive of his remembrance of his American friends, than any letters can convey. That the principles of America opened the Bastille is not to be doubted; and therefore the key comes to the right place.

To George Washington, May 1, 1790

I have wished to see America the *Mother Church* of government.

To James Monroe, September 10, 1794

America has the high honor and happiness of being the first nation that gave to the world the example of forming written constitutions by conventions elected expressly for the purpose, and of improving them by the same procedure, as time and experience shall show necessary. Government in other nations, vainly calling themselves civilized, has been established by bloodshed. Not a drop of blood has been shed in the United States in consequence of establishing constitutions and governments by her own peaceful system. The silent vote, or the simple *yea or nay*, is more powerful than the bayonet, and decides the strength of numbers without a blow.

To the Citizens of Pennsylvania on the Proposal
for Calling a Convention, 1805

American Foreign Relations

❧ ❧

As Europe is our market for trade, we ought to form no partial connection with any part of it. It is the true interest of America to steer clear of European contentions.

Common Sense, 1776

America, remote from all the wrangling world, may live at ease. Bounded by the ocean and backed by the wilderness, what hath she to fear, but her GOD?

The Forester's Letters, 1776

American Revolution

❧ ❧

The sun never shined on a cause of greater worth. 'Tis not the affair of a city, a country, a province, or a kingdom, but of a continent—of at least one eighth part of the habitable globe. 'Tis not the concern of a day, a year, or an age; posterity are virtually involved in the contest, and will be more or less affected, even to the end of time, by the proceedings now. Now is the seed time of continental union, faith and honor. The least fracture now will be like a name engraved with the point of a pin on the tender rind of a young oak; the wound will enlarge with the tree, and posterity read it in full grown characters.

Common Sense, 1776

Small islands not capable of protecting themselves, are the proper objects for kingdoms to take under their care; but there is something very absurd, in supposing a continent to be perpetually governed by an island. In no instance hath nature made the satellite larger than its primary planet, and as England and America, with respect to each other, reverses the common order of nature, it is evident they belong to different systems: England to Europe, America to itself.

Common Sense, 1776

I am not induced by motives of pride, party, or resentment to espouse the doctrine of separation and independence; I am clearly, positively, and conscientiously persuaded that it is the true interest of this continent to be so; that every thing short of that is mere patchwork, that it can afford no lasting felicity,—that it is leaving the sword to our children, and shrinking back at a time, when, a little more, a little farther, would have rendered this continent the glory of the earth.

Common Sense, 1776

The present time, likewise, is that peculiar time, which never happens to a nation but once, *viz.* the time of forming itself into a government. Most nations have let slip the opportunity, and by that means have been compelled to receive laws from their conquerors, instead of making laws for themselves. . . . but from the errors of other nations, let us learn wisdom, and lay hold of the present opportunity — *To begin government at the right end.*

Common Sense, 1776

Until an independence is declared, the Continent will feel itself like a man who continues putting off some unpleasant business from day to day, yet knows it must be done, hates to set about it, wishes it over, and is continually haunted with the thoughts of its necessity.

Common Sense, 1776

Let it be told to the future world, that in the depth of winter, when nothing but hope and virtue could survive, that the city and the country, alarmed at one common danger, came forth to meet and to repulse it. Say not, that thousands are gone, turn out your tens of thousands; throw not the burthen of the day upon Providence, but *"show your faith by your works,"* that GOD may bless you. It matters not where you live, or what rank of life you hold, the evil or the blessing will reach you all. The far and the near, the home counties and the back, the rich and the poor, shall suffer or rejoice alike. The heart that feels not now, is dead. The blood of his children shall curse his cowardice, who shrinks back at a time when a little might have saved the whole, and made *them* happy. I love the man that can smile in trouble, that can gather strength from distress, and grow brave by reflection. 'Tis the business of little minds to shrink; but he whose heart is firm, and whose conscience approves his conduct, will pursue his principles unto death.

The American Crisis, 1776

After the coolest reflections on the matter, *this must* be allowed, that Britain was too jealous of America, to govern it justly; too ignorant of it, to govern it well; and too distant from it, to govern it at all.

The American Crisis, 1777

The final superiority of America over every attempt which an island might make to conquer her, was as naturally marked in the constitution of things, as the future ability of a giant over a dwarf is delineated in his features while an infant.

Common Sense on George III's Speech, 1782

"The times that tried men's souls," are over—and the greatest and completest revolution the world ever knew is gloriously and happily accomplished.

The Crisis, 1783

The revolution of America presented in politics what was only theory in mechanics.

Rights of Man, II, 1792

The independence of America, considered merely as a separation from England, would have been a matter but of little importance, had it not been accompanied by a revolution in the principles and practices of government. She made a stand, not for herself only, but for the world.

Rights of Man, II, 1792

Ancestry

No reflection ought to be made on any man on account of birth, provided that his manners rises decently with his circumstances, and that he affects not to forget the level he came from; when he does, he ought to be led back and shown the mortifying picture of originality.

Four Letters on Interesting Subjects, 1776

Anger

There are men too, who have not virtue enough to be angry.

The Forester's Letters, 1776

A mind disarmed of its rage, feels no pleasure in contemplating a frantic quarrel. Sickness of thought . . . leaves no ability for enjoyment, no relish for resentment; and though like a man in a fit, you feel not the injury of the struggle, nor distinguish between strength and disease, the weakness will nevertheless be proportioned to the violence, and the sense of pain increase with the recovery.

The Crisis, 1780

Anonymous Publications

A man ought to be ashamed to publish any thing which he is ashamed to own.

Candid and Critical Remarks on a Letter Signed Ludlow, 1777

Anti-Isolationism

It is best mankind should mix. There is ever something to learn, either of manners or principle; and it is by a free communication, without regard to domestic matters, that friendship is to be extended and prejudice destroyed all over the world.

Letter to the Abbé Raynal, 1782

Appropriations

Public money ought to be touched with the most scrupulous consciousness of honor.

Rights of Man, II, 1792

Aristocracy

The more aristocracy appeared, the more it was despised; there was a visible imbecility and want of intellects in the majority, a sort of *je ne sais quoi*, that while it affected to be more than citizen, was less than man. It lost ground from contempt more than from hatred; and was rather jeered at as an ass, than dreaded as a lion. This is the general character of aristocracy, or what are called Nobles or Nobility, or rather No-ability, in all countries.

Rights of Man, I, 1791

Nature is often giving to the world some extraordinary men who arrive at fame by merit and universal consent, such as Aristotle, Socrates, Plato, etc. They were truly great or noble. But when government sets up a manufactory of nobles, it is as absurd as if she undertook to manufacture wise men. Her nobles are all counterfeits.

Dissertation on First Principles of Government, 1795

The first aristocrats in all countries were brigands. Those of later times, sycophants.

Dissertation on First Principles of Government, 1795

Armies

An army, though it is the defense of a state, is at the same time the child of a country, and must be provided for in every thing.
The Crisis, 1777; *Common Sense on Financing the War*, 1782

An army in a city can never be a conquering army. The situation admits only a defence.

The Crisis, 1778

Possessing yourselves of towns is not conquest, but convenience, and in which you will one day or other be trepanned.

The Crisis, 1778

Artifice and Cunning

The man who resorts to artifice and cunning, instead of standing on the firm and open ground of principle can easily be found out.

Letters to Morgan Lewis, 1807

The Arts

Every principal art has some science for its parent, though the person who mechanically performs the work does not always, and but very seldom, perceives the connection.

Age of Reason, I, 1794

Assertions

A man ought never to leave an assertion to shift for itself. It is like turning out a sickly infant to beg a home in other people's houses.

A Friend to Rhode-Island and the Union, 1783

Astonishment

Wise men are astonished at foolish things, and other people at wise ones.

Rights of Man, I, 1791

Avarice

While avarice and ambition have a place in the heart of man, the weak will become a prey to the strong.

Thoughts on Defensive War, 1775

Though avarice will preserve a man from being necessitously poor, it generally makes him too timorous to be wealthy.

Common Sense, 1776

Men whose political principles are founded on avarice, are beyond the reach of reason.

The American Crisis, 1777

Avarice is a fixed uniform passion. It neither abates of its vigor nor changes its object; and the reason why it does not is founded in the nature of things, for wealth has not a rival where avarice is a ruling passion. One beauty may excel another, and extinguish from the mind of a man the pictured remembrance of a former one: But wealth is the phoenix of avarice, and therefore cannot seek a new object, because there is not another in the world.

The Crisis Extraordinary, 1780

Bad Causes

❧

A bad cause will ever be supported by bad means and bad men.

The American Crisis, 1777

Bankruptcy

❧

Nothing is more common than to see the bankrupt of today a man of credit but the day before; yet no sooner is the real state of his affairs known, than every body can see that he had been insolvent long before.

Decline and Fall of the English System of Finance, 1796

Banks

❧

Public Banks are reckoned among the honors, privileges and advantages of a free people, and are never found among those under a despotic government.

On the Affairs of Pennsylvania, 1786

Beginnings

Every thing must have had a beginning, and the fog of time and antiquity should be penetrated to discover it.

Rights of Man, I, 1791

The shortest and most effectual remedy is to begin anew.

Rights of Man, II, 1792

The probability is always greater against a thing beginning, than of proceeding after it has begun.

Rights of Man, II, 1792

Every art and science has some point, or alphabet, at which the study of that art or science begins, and by the assistance of which the progress is facilitated.

Dissertation on First Principles of Government, 1795

Beliefs

A multiplication of beliefs acts as a division of belief, and in proportion as any thing is divided it is weakened.

Age of Reason, I, 1794

Benefit to Society

A substantial good drawn from a real evil, is of the same benefit to society, as if drawn from a virtue.

The American Crisis, 1777

The Bible

❧ ☙

When we contemplate the immensity of that Being, who directs and governs the incomprehensible WHOLE, of which the utmost ken of human sight can discover but a part, we ought to feel shame at calling such paltry stories the word of God.

Age of Reason, I, 1794

When I see throughout the greatest part of this book, scarcely any thing but a history of the grossest vices, and a collection of the most paltry and contemptible tales, I cannot dishonor my Creator by calling it by his name.

Age of Reason, I, 1794

People in general know not what wickedness there is in this pretended word of God. Brought up in habits of superstition, they take it for granted, that the bible is true, and that it is good. They permit themselves not to doubt of it; and they carry the ideas they form of the benevolence of the Almighty to the book which they have been taught to believe was written by his authority. Good heavens, it is quite another thing! It is a book of lies, wickedness, and blasphemy; for what can be greater blasphemy than to ascribe the wickedness of man to the orders of the Almighty.

Age of Reason, II, 1795

Bills of Rights

❧ ☙

A Declaration of Rights is, by reciprocity, a Declaration of Duties also. Whatever is my right as a man, is also the right of another; and it becomes my duty to guarantee, as well as to possess.

Rights of Man, I, 1791

A declaration of rights is not a creation of them, nor a donation of them. It is a manifest of the principle by which they exist, followed by a detail of what the rights are; for every civil right has a natural right for its foundation.

Dissertation on First Principles of Government, 1795

Blessings in Disguise

❧ ❦

What lately appeared to us misfortunes, were only blessings in disguise.

The American Crisis, 1777

Boundaries

❧ ❦

Suppose we draw a circle around a man, and address him thus: "You cannot step beyond this boundary, for, if you did, you would be swallowed up in an abyss." As long as the terror with which these words have inspired him continues, he will stay where he is. But if, by some lucky accident, he places one foot beyond the line, the other will come after it.

Answers to Four Questions on Legislative and Executive Powers, 1791

Breadth of Perspective

❧ ❦

But perhaps there is something in the extent of countries which among the generality of people, insensibly communicates extension to the mind. The soul of an Islander in the native State, seems bounded by the foggy confines of the water's edge, and all beyond, affords to him matter only for profit or curiosity, not for friendship. His island is to him his world, and fixed to that his every thing centers in it; while those, who are inhabitants of a continent, by casting their eye over a large field, takes in likewise a larger intellectual circuit, and thus approaching nearer to an acquaintance with the universe, their atmosphere of thought is extended, and their liberality fills a wider space. In short, our minds seem to be measured by countries when we are men, as they are by places, when we are children, and until something happens to disentangle us from the prejudice, we serve under it without perceiving it.

In addition to this, it may be remarked, that men who study any universal science, the principles of which are universally known, or admitted, and applied without distinction to the common benefit of all countries, obtain thereby a larger share of philanthropy than those who only study national arts and improvements. Natural philosophy, mathematics and astronomy, carry the mind from the country to the creation, and give it a fitness suited to the extent. It was not Newton's honor, neither could it be his pride, that he was an Englishman, but that he was a philosopher: The Heavens had liberated him from the prejudices of an island, and science had expanded his soul as boundless as his studies.

The Crisis, 1780

British Incompetence

On our part, in order to know, at any time, what the British government will do, we have only to find out what they ought NOT to do, and this last will be their conduct.

The Crisis, 1782

That a country has a right to be as foolish as it pleases, has been proved by the practice of England for many years past.

Commerce with Britain and the Necessity of Union, 1783

Calmness

Even calmness has the power of stunning when it opens too instantly upon us.

The Crisis, 1783

Calumny

Calumny is a species of Treachery that ought to be punished as well as any other kind of Treachery. It is a private vice productive of a public evil, because it is possible to irritate men into disaffection by continual calumny who never intended to be disaffected.

Letter to Citizen Danton, May 6, 1793

Calumny becomes harmless and defeats itself when it attempts to act upon too large a scale.

Letter to Citizen Danton, May 6, 1793

Calumny is a vice of a curious constitution. Trying to kill it keeps it alive; leave it to itself and it will die a natural death.

Letters to Morgan Lewis, 1807

Cause and Effect

Every circumstance is pregnant with some natural effect, upon which intentions and opinions have no influence; and the political error lies in misjudging what the effect will be.

Age of Reason, I, 1794

Censure

Censure is but awkwardly softened by apology.

To George Washington, August 3, 1796

Ceremony

Ceremony, and even, silence, from whatever motive they may arise, have a hurtful tendency, when they give the least degree of countenance to base and wicked performances.

Common Sense, 1776

Change

Change of times adds propriety to new measures.

The Pennsylvania Magazine, 1775

The circumstances of the world are continually changing, and the opinions of men change also.

Rights of Man, I, 1791

Character

Difference of constitution, temper, habit of speaking and many other things will go a great way in fixing the outward character of a man, yet simple honesty may remain at bottom.

The American Crisis, 1777

Characters are tender and valuable things; they are more than life to a man of sensibility, and are not to be made the sport of interest, or the sacrifice of incendiary malice.

Pennsylvania Packet, December 31, 1778

Character, like trade, is subject to bankruptcy.

Pennsylvania Packet, February 16, 1779

Character is to us, in our present circumstances, of more importance than interest.

The Crisis, 1782

There are cases in which it is as impossible to restore character to life, as it is to recover the dead. It is a phoenix that can expire but once, and from whose ashes there is no resurrection.

To the Earl of Shelburne, 1782

Character is much easier kept than recovered, and that man, if any such there be, who, from any sinister views, or littleness of soul, lends unseen his hand to injure it, contrives a wound it will never be in his power to heal.

The Crisis, 1783

The name by which a man is called is of itself but an empty thing. It is worth and character alone which can render him valuable, for without these, kings, and lords, and presidents, are but jingling names.

To Mr. Secretary Dundas, 1792

Imprisonment with preservation of character, is preferable to liberty with disgrace.

To James Monroe, September 10, 1794

It is curious to observe, how the appearance of characters will change, whilst the root that produces them remains the same.

To George Washington, February 22, 1795

As a general rule, we may take it for granted, and that with as few exceptions as any general rule will admit of, that *private character is the foundation of public character*, and that where public character is uniformly honorable and upright, and that for a great length of time, the private character will be found the same.

A Spark from the Altar of '76, 1805

It is, perhaps, a bold sentiment but it is a true one, that a *just man, when attacked, should not defend himself.* His conduct will do it for him, and Time will put his detractors under his feet.

A Spark from the Altar of '76, 1805

A man must feel his character exceedingly vulnerable, who can suppose that anything said about him, or against him, can endamage him.

Letters to Morgan Lewis, 1807

Charity

There are, in every country, some magnificent charities established by individuals. It is, however, but little that any individual can do, when the whole extent of the misery to be relieved is considered. He may satisfy his conscience, but not his heart. He may give all that he has, and that all will relieve but little. It is only by organizing civilization upon such principles as to act like a system of pulleys, that the whole weight of misery can be removed.

Agrarian Justice, 1797

Checks and Balances

As the greater weight will always carry up the less, and as all the wheels of a machine are put in motion by one, it only remains to know which power in the constitution has the most weight, for that will govern; and though the others, or a part of them, may clog, or, as the phrase is, check the rapidity of its motion, yet so long as they cannot stop it, their endeavors will be ineffectual; the first moving power will at last have its way, and what it wants in speed is supplied by time.

Common Sense, 1776

Choices

❧ ❧

The power of choosing is an agreeable thing to the mind.

The Crisis Extraordinary, 1780

If the one be demonstrably better than the other that difference directs our choice; but if one of them should be so absolutely false as not to have a right of existence the matter settles itself at once; because a negative proved on one thing, where two only are offered, and one must be accepted, amounts to an affirmative on the other.

Dissertation on First Principles of Government, 1795

Christianity

❧ ❧

The church has set up a system of religion very contradictory to the character of the person whose name it bears. It has set up a religion of pomp and of revenue in pretended imitation of a person whose life was humility and poverty.

Age of Reason, I, 1794

As to the christian system of faith, it appears to me as a species of atheism; a sort of religious denial of God. It professes to believe in a man rather than in God. It is a compound made up chiefly of manism with but little deism. It introduces between man and his maker an opaque body which it calls a redeemer; as the moon introduces her opaque self between the earth and the sun, and it produces by this means a religious or an irreligious eclipse of light. It has put the whole orb of reason into shade.

The effect of this obscurity has been that of turning every thing upside down, and representing it in reverse; and among the revolutions it has thus magically produced, it has made a revolution in Theology.

That which is now called natural philosophy, embracing the whole circle of science, of which astronomy occupies the chief place, is the study of the works of God and of the power and wisdom of God in his works, and is the true theology.

As to the theology that is now studied in its place, it is the study of human opinions and of human fancies *concerning* God. It is not the study of God himself in the works that he has made, but in the works or writings that man has made; and it is not among the least of the mischiefs that the christian system has done to the world, that it has abandoned the original and beautiful system of theology, like a beautiful innocent to distress and reproach, to make room for the hag of superstition.

Age of Reason, I, 1794

Citizenship

❧ ❦

Our citizenship in the united states is our national character. Our citizenship in any particular state is only our local distinction. By the latter we are known at home, by the former to the world. Our great title is, AMERICAN; our inferior one varies with the place.

The Crisis, 1783

Every man in America stands in a two-fold order of citizenship. He is a citizen of the State he lives in, and of the United States; and without justly and truly supporting his citizenship in the latter, he will inevitably sacrifice the former. By his rank in the one, he is made secure with his neighbors; by the other, with the world. The one protects his domestic safety and property from internal robbers and injustice; the other his foreign and remote property from piracy and invasion, and puts him on a rank with other nations. Certainly then the one, like the other, must not and cannot be trusted to plea-sure and caprice, lest, in the display of local authority, we forget the great line that made us great, and must keep us so.

A Friend to Rhode-Island and the Union, 1783

Civil Rights

❧ ☙

Man did not enter into society to become *worse* than he was before, nor to have less rights than he had before, but to have those rights better secured. His natural rights are the foundation of all his civil rights.

Rights of Man, I, 1791

Civilization

❧ ☙

Whether the state that is proudly, perhaps erroneously, called civi-lization, has most promoted or most injured the general happiness of man, is a question that may be strongly contested. On one side, the spectator is dazzled by splendid appearances; on the other he is shocked by extremes of wretchedness; both of which he has erected. The most affluent and the most miserable of the human race are to be found in the countries that are called civilized.

Agrarian Justice, 1797

Clemency

❧ ☙

Success and power are the only situations in which clemency can be shown.

Common Sense on George III's Speech, 1782

Closed-Mindedness

❧ ❧

It is folly to argue against determined hardness; eloquence may strike the ear, and the language of sorrow draw forth the tear of compassion, but nothing can reach the heart that is steeled with prejudice.

The American Crisis, 1776

Closing a Letter

❧ ❧

I am always distressed at closing a letter, because it seems like taking leave of my friends after a parting conversation.

To Kitty Nicholson Few, January 6, 1789

Commerce

❧ ❧

Commerce diminishes the spirit, both of patriotism and military defense.

Common Sense, 1776

Commerce is no other than the traffic of two individuals, multiplied on a scale of numbers; and by the same rule that nature intended the intercourse of two, she intended that of all. For this purpose she has distributed the materials of manufactures and commerce, in various and distant parts of a nation and of the world; and as they cannot be procured by war so cheaply or so commodiously as by commerce, she has rendered the latter the means of extirpating the former.

Rights of Man, II, 1792

The great support of commerce consists in the balance being a level of benefits among all nations.

Rights of Man, II, 1792

Comparison

The estimation of all things is by comparison.

Rights of Man, I, 1791

Compassion

It is the nature of compassion to associate with misfortune.

To Sir Guy Carleton, 1782; Rights of Man, II, 1792

My compassion for the unfortunate, whether friend or enemy, is . . . lively and sincere.

Speech to the French National Convention, January 15, 1793

Confidence

It is to me, and must to every sensible mind, a pleasure when men having the same *public good* in view, and capable, according to their several talents, to promote it, come to understand and place confidence in each other. Good opinion is the true foundation of acquaintance and when that takes place good designs may be promoted with the greatest ease.

To Robert Morris, February 20, 1782

Wherever there is a want of satisfaction there must necessarily be a want of confidence.

Thoughts on the Establishment of a Mint in the United States, 1790

Confidence can never take place . . . where mystery and secrecy on one side, is opposed to candor and openness on the other.

Rights of Man, II, 1792

Conquest

✤

Conquest may be effected under the pretense of friendship.

Common Sense, 1776

Conscience

✤

Were the impulses of conscience clear, uniform, and irresistibly obeyed, man would need no other lawgiver.

Common Sense, 1776

Consequences

✤

The cheat lies in putting the consequences for the cause.

The Forester's Letters, 1776

There are certain circumstances that will produce certain events whether men think of them or not. The events do not depend upon thinking, but are the natural consequence of acting.

Public Good, 1780

If men will give challenges, they must expect consequences.

Rights of Man, I, 1791

Consistency

✣

Consistency has some pretensions to character.

Pennsylvania Packet, March 2, 1779

Man, with respect to all those matters, is more a creature of consistency than he is aware, or that governments would wish him to believe.

Rights of Man, II, 1792

Consolation

✣

There is, perhaps, no condition from which a man, conscious of his own uprightness, cannot derive consolation; for it is in itself a consolation for him to find, that he can bear that condition with calmness and fortitude.

To George Washington, August 3, 1796

Conspiracy

✣

Conspiracy is quick of suspicion.

To the People of France and the French Armies, 1797

It is exceedingly difficult, and next to impossible, to conduct a conspiracy, and still more so to give it success, in a popular government.

To the People of France and the French Armies, 1797

Constitutional Amendments

❦

All that wisdom can do at present is to see that no future improvement shall be obstructed. . . . To fetter ourselves would be folly; to fetter posterity would be usurpation; we must do nothing that impedes progress. If man had any rights over posterity, our rights would have been ruined long ago. . . . I wish to benefit our posterity, let us leave them liberty as a bequest, and, along with it, the encouragement of good example. Everything that deserves imitation is sure to be imitated. If our institutions are intrinsically admirable, posterity will assimilate them, and there will be no necessity for us to try to exercise our authority over our descendants.

Answers to Four Questions on Legislative and Executive Powers, 1791

Government has no right to make itself a party in any debate respecting the principles or modes of forming, or of changing, constitutions. It is not for the benefit of those who exercise the powers of government, that constitutions, and the governments issuing from them, are established. In all those matters, the right of judging and acting are in those who pay, and not in those who receive.

Rights of Man, II, 1792

That as government in America is founded on the representative system, any error in the first essay could be reformed by the same quiet and rational process by which the constitution was formed; and that, either by the generation then living, or by those who were to succeed. If ever America lose sight of this principle, she will no longer be the *land of liberty*. The father will become the assassin of the rights of the son, and his descendants be a race of slaves.

To the Citizens of the United States, 1802

Constitutional Provisions

❧

The weaker any cord is, the less will it bear to be stretched, and the worse is the policy to stretch it, unless it is intended to break it.

Rights of Man, I, 1791

Constitutions

❧

A government of our own is our natural right: And when a man seriously reflects on the precariousness of human affairs, he will become convinced, that it is infinitely wiser and safer, to form a constitution of our own in a cool deliberate manner, while we have it in our own power, than to trust such an interesting event to time and chance.

Common Sense, 1776

Can we but leave posterity with a settled form of government, an independent constitution of its own, the purchase at any price will be cheap.

Common Sense, 1776

A charter is to be understood as a bond of solemn obligation, which the whole enters into, to support the right of every separate part, whether of religion, personal freedom, or property.

Common Sense, 1776

A Constitution, and a form of government, are frequently confounded together, and spoken of as synonymous things; whereas they are not only different, but are established for different purposes: All countries have some form of government, but few, or perhaps none, have truly a Constitution. The form of government in England is by a king, lords and commons; but if you ask an Englishman what he means when he speaks of the English Constitution, he is unable to give you any answer. The truth is, the English have no fixed Constitution.

Four Letters on Interesting Subjects, 1776

A Constitution, when completed, resolves the two following questions: First, What shall the form of government be? And secondly, What shall be its power? And the last of these two is far more material than the first.

Four Letters on Interesting Subjects, 1776

Let the form of government be what it may, in this, or other provinces, so long as it answers the purpose of the people, and they approve it, they will be happy under it.

Four Letters on Interesting Subjects, 1776

There can be no fixed principles of government, or any thing like [a] Constitution in a Country where the government can alter itself, or one part of it supply the other.

To Thomas Jefferson, February 16, 1789

A constitution is a thing *antecedent* to a government, and a government is only the creature of a constitution. The constitution of a country is not the act of its government, but of the people constituting a government. . . . A constitution . . . is to a government what the laws made afterwards by that government are to a court of judicature. The court of judicature does not make the laws, neither can it alter them; it only acts in conformity to the laws made; and the government is in like manner governed by the constitution.

Rights of Man, I, 1791

The American constitutions were to liberty, what a grammar is to language: they define its parts of speech, and practically construct them into syntax.

Rights of Man, I, 1791

A constitution is not the act of a government, but of a people constituting a government; and government without a constitution, is power without a right.

Rights of Man, II, 1792

A constitution is the property of a nation, and not of those who exercise the government.

Rights of Man, II, 1792

It [i.e., the Pennsylvania constitution of 1776] was the political bible of the state.

Rights of Man, II, 1792

The laws which are enacted by government, control men only as individuals, but the nation, through its constitution, controls the whole government.

Rights of Man, II, 1792

In forming a constitution, it is first necessary to consider what are the ends for which government is necessary? Secondly, what are the best means, and the least expensive, for accomplishing those ends?

Rights of Man, II, 1792

It is the nature and intention of a constitution to *prevent governing by party*, by establishing a common principle that shall limit and control the power and impulse of party, and that says to all parties, *Thus far shalt thou go and no further*. But in the absence of a constitution, men look entirely to party; and instead of principle governing party, party governs principle.

Dissertation on First Principles of Government, 1795

A constitution embraces two distinct parts or objects, the *principle* and the *practice*; and it is not only an essential, but an indispensable provision, that the practice should emanate from and accord with the principle.

Speech to the French National Convention, 1795

A constitution is the act of the people in their original character of sovereignty. A government is a creature of the constitution; it is produced and brought into existence by it. A constitution defines and limits the powers of the government it creates. It therefore follows, as a natural and also a logical result, that the governmental exercise of any power not authorized by the constitution is an assumed power, and therefore illegal.

Constitutions, Governments, and Charters, 1805

Contempt

Government with insolence, is despotism; but when contempt is added, it becomes worse; and to pay for contempt, is the excess of slavery.

Rights of Man, I, 1791

Copyright

It may with propriety be marked, that in all countries where literature is protected, and it never can flourish where it is not, the works of an author are his legal property; and to treat letters in any other light than this, is to banish them from the country, or strangle them in the birth.

Letter to the Abbé Raynal, 1782

Correspondence

When there is no matter to write upon, a letter is not worth the trouble of receiving and reading, and while any thing, which is to be the subject of a letter, is in suspense, it is difficult to write, and perhaps best to let it alone — *"least said is soonest mended,"* and nothing said requires no mending.

To Thomas Jefferson, September 9, 1788

Corroboration

I lay it down as a position which cannot be controverted; First, that the *agreement* of all the parts of a story does not prove that story to be true, because the parts may agree and the whole may be false: Secondly, that the *disagreement* of the parts of a story proves the *whole cannot be true*. The agreement does not prove truth, but the disagreement proves falsehood positively.

Age of Reason, II, 1795

Corruption

There is something in corruption, which, like a jaundiced eye, transfers the color of itself to the object it looks upon, and sees every thing stained and impure.

The Crisis, 1778

Courage

Most men have more courage than they know of, and that a little at first is enough to begin with.

The American Crisis, 1777

Courtiers

Notwithstanding appearances, there is not any description of men that despise monarchy so much as courtiers. . . . The difference between a republican and a courtier with respect to monarchy is, that the one opposes monarchy believing it to be something, and the other laughs at it knowing it to be nothing.

Rights of Man, I, 1791

Covetousness

The love of gold and silver may produce covetousness, but covetousness, when not connected with dishonesty, is not properly a vice. It is frugality run to an extreme.

Dissertations on Government, 1786

Cowardice

By perseverance and fortitude we have the prospect of a glorious issue; by cowardice and submission, the sad choice of a variety of evils.

The American Crisis, 1776

The Creation

Every nation of people has been world-makers [i.e., developers of a theory of the Creation].

Age of Reason, I, 1794

It is only in the CREATION that all our ideas and conceptions of a *word of God* can unite.

Age of Reason, I, 1794

The creation is the bible of the deist. He there reads, in the hand writing of the Creator himself, the certainty of his existence, and the immutability of his power; and all other bibles and testaments are to him forgeries.

Age of Reason, I, 1794

It is necessary that we refer to the bible of the creation. The principles we discover there are eternal and of divine origin. They are the foundation of all the science that exists in the world, and must be the foundation of theology.

Age of Reason, II, 1795

Do we want to know what GOD is? Search not written or printed books, but the Scripture called the *creation*.

A Discourse at the Society of Theophilanthropists, 1797; To Samuel Adams, Washington, January 1, 1803; *Age of Reason*, I, 1794 (slight variation)

Credit

❦

Credit is not money, and therefore it is not pay, neither can it be put in the place of money in the end. It is only the means of getting into debt, not the means of getting out.

Prospects on the Rubicon, 1787

Credulity

❧

Credulity is wealth while credulity lasts, and credit is, in a thousand instances, the child of credulity.

Prospects on the Rubicon, 1787

Credulity is not a crime.

Age of Reason, I, 1794

Credulity, however, is not a crime; but it becomes criminal by resisting conviction. It is strangling in the womb of the conscience the efforts it makes to ascertain truth. We should never force belief upon ourselves in any thing.

Age of Reason, II, 1795

Creed

❧

I am neither farmer, manufacturer, mechanic, merchant nor shopkeeper. I believe, however, I am of the first class. I am a *Farmer of thoughts*.

Letter to Henry Laurens, 1778

I have ever kept a clear head and an upright heart, and am not afraid of being replied to. I never took up a matter without fully believing it to be right, and never yet failed in proving it so.

Philadelphia *Freeman's Journal*, May 1, 1782

It was the cause of America that made me an author.

The Crisis, 1783

Independence is my happiness, and I view things as they are, without regard to place or person; my country is the world, and my religion is to do good.

Rights of Man, II, 1792

I believe in one God, and no more; and I hope for happiness beyond this life.

Age of Reason, I, 1794

My own mind is my own church.

Age of Reason, I, 1794

. . . the first article of every man's creed, and of every nation's creed, that has any creed at all. *I believe in God.*

To Samuel Adams, Washington, January 1, 1803

I have lived an honest and useful life to mankind; my time has been spent in doing good, and I die in perfect composure and resignation to the will of my Creator, God.

The Last Will and Testament of Thomas Paine, January 18, 1809

Crimes of the Heart

Errors, or caprices of the temper, can be pardoned and forgotten; but a cold, deliberate crime of the heart . . . is not to be washed away.

To George Washington, February 22, 1795

Crisis

These are the times that try men's souls: The summer soldier and the sunshine patriot will, in this crisis, shrink from the service of his country; but he that stands it NOW, deserves the love and thanks of man and woman.

The American Crisis, 1776

The nearer any disease approaches to a crisis, the nearer it is to a cure: Danger and deliverance make their advances together, and it is only at the last push, that one or the other takes the lead.

The American Crisis, 1777

Cunning

❧ ❧

The cunning of the fox is as murderous as the violence of the wolf; and we ought to guard equally against both.

The American Crisis, 1776

Curiosity

❧ ❧

Of all the innocent passions which actuate the human mind, there is none more universally prevalent than curiosity. It reaches all mankind, and in matters which concern us, or concern us not, it alike provokes in us a desire to know.

Common Sense on George III's Speech, 1782

The Dark Ages

❧ ❧

It is owing to this long interregnum of science, *and to no other cause,* that we have now to look back through a vast chasm of many hundred years to the respectable characters we call the ancients. Had the progression of knowledge gone on proportionably with the stock that before existed, that chasm would have been filled up with characters rising superior in knowledge to each other; and those ancients, we now so much admire, would have appeared respectably in the back ground of the scene. But the christian system laid all waste; and if we take our stand about the beginning of the sixteenth century, we look back through that long chasm, to the times of the ancients, as over a vast sandy desert, in which not a shrub appears to intercept the vision to the fertile hills beyond.

Age of Reason, I, 1794

Dearness

❦

What we obtain too cheap, we esteem too lightly:—'Tis dearness only that gives every thing its value.

The American Crisis, 1776

Death

❦

However men may differ in their ideas of grandeur or of government here, the grave is nevertheless a perfect republic.

The American Crisis, 1778

Death is not the monarch of the dead, but of the dying. The moment he obtains a conquest he loses a subject.

The American Crisis, 1778

It is the nature of man to die, and he will continue to die as long as he continues to be born.

Rights of Man, I, 1791

Nothing, they say, is more certain than death, and nothing more uncertain than the time of dying.

Decline and Fall of the English System of Finance, 1796

Death Penalty

※ ⁊

It has been already proposed to abolish the punishment of death; . . .
This cause must find its advocates in every corner, where enlightened
Politicians, and lovers of Humanity exist.

Speech to the French National Convention, January 15, 1793

Deception

※ ⁊

To deceive is to destroy.

The Crisis, 1778

A man will pass better through the world with a thousand open errors upon his back, than in being detected in *one* sly falsehood. When
one is detected, a thousand are suspected.

To George Washington, February 22, 1795

Defense

※ ⁊

Our methods of defense, ought to improve with our increase of
property.

Common Sense, 1776

Deism

The true deist has but one Deity; and his religion consists in contemplating the power, wisdom, and benignity of the Deity in his works, and in endeavoring to imitate him in every thing moral, scientifical, and mechanical.

Age of Reason, I, 1794

It is a duty incumbent on every true deist, that he vindicates the moral justice of God against the calumnies of the bible.

Age of Reason, II, 1795

Is it not more safe that we stop ourselves at the plain, pure, and unmixed belief of one God, which is Deism, than that we commit ourselves on an ocean of improbable, irrational, indecent and contradictory tales [i.e., the Bible]?

Age of Reason, II, 1795

The only religion that has not been invented, and that has in it every evidence of divine originality, is pure and simple deism.

Age of Reason, II, 1795

Deliberateness

Slow and sure is sound work.

The American Crisis, 1778

Democracy

❦

The greatest characters the world have known, have rose on the democratic floor. Aristocracy has not been able to keep a proportionate pace with democracy.

Rights of Man, I, 1791

The strength of government consists in the interest the people have in supporting it. . . . Mere politicians of the old school may talk of alliances, but the strongest of all alliances is that which the mildness, wisdom, and justice of government form, unperceived, with the people it governs. It grows in the mind with the secrecy and fidelity of love, and reposes on its own energy. Make it the interest of the people to live in a state of government, and they will protect that which protects them. But when they are with taxes for which they can see no cause, their confidence in such government withers away, and they laugh at the energy that attempts to restore it. Their cry then is, as in the time of the terror (*"not to your tents, O! Israel*), but to the NEXT ELECTION O! CITIZENS." It is thus the *representative system corrects wrongs and preserves rights.*

*Remarks on Gouverneur Morris' Funeral Oration
on Alexander Hamilton*, 1804

Despair

❦

While despair is preying on the mind, time and its effects are preying on despair; and certain it is, the dismal vision will fade away, and *Forgetfulness*, with her sister Ease, will change the scene.

Forgetfulness, 1794

Despotism

No country can be called *free* which is governed by an absolute power; and it matters not whether it be an absolute royal power or an absolute legislative power, as the consequences will be the same to the people.

Four Letters on Interesting Subjects, 1776

A despotic government knows no principle but will. Whatever the sovereign wills to do, the government admits him the inherent right, and the uncontrolled power of doing. He is restrained by no fixed rule of right and wrong.

Dissertations on Government, 1786

A casual discontinuance of the *practice* of despotism, is not a discontinuance of its *principles*; the former depends on the virtue of the individual who is in immediate possession of the power; the latter, on the virtue and fortitude of the nation.

Rights of Man, I, 1791

Every place has its Bastille, and every Bastille its despot.

Rights of Man, I, 1791

To reason with despots is throwing reason away.

Letter to the People of France, 1792

The strength and powers of despotism consist wholly in the fear of resisting it.

Rights of Man, II, 1792

The preclusion of consent is despotism.

Dissertation on First Principles of Government, 1795

Despotic government supports itself by abject civilization, in which debasement of the human mind, and wretchedness in the mass of the people, are the chief criterians. Such governments consider man merely as an animal; that the exercise of intellectual faculty is not his privilege; that he has nothing to do with the laws, but to obey them; and they politically depend more upon breaking the spirit of the people by poverty, than they fear enraging it by desperation.

Agrarian Justice, 1797

Destiny, Shaping of

Man cannot, properly speaking, make circumstances for his purpose, but he always has it in his power to improve them when they occur.

Rights of Man, I, 1791

Diatribes

When the tongue or the pen is let loose in a frenzy of passion, it is the man, and not the subject that becomes exhausted.

Rights of Man, I, 1791

Dignity

When once the mind loses the sense of its own dignity, it loses, likewise, the ability of judging of it in another.

Letter to the Abbé Raynal, 1782

Diplomats

The diplomatic character is of itself the narrowest sphere of society that man can act in. It forbids intercourse by a reciprocity of suspicion; and a Diplomatic is a sort of unconnected atom, continually repelling and repelled.

Rights of Man, I, 1791

Disarmament

Could the peaceable principle of the Quakers be universally established, arms and the art of war would be wholly extirpated. But we live not in a world of angels. The reign of Satan is not ended; neither are we to expect to be defended by miracles. . . . I am thus far a Quaker, that I would gladly agree with all the world to lay aside the use of arms, and settle matters by negotiation; but unless the whole will, the matter ends, and I take up my musket and thank heaven he has put it in my power.

Thoughts on Defensive War, 1775

The balance of power is the scale of peace. The same balance would be preserved were all the world destitute of arms, for all would be alike; but since some *will not*, others *dare not* lay them aside. And while a single nation refuses to lay them down, it is proper that all should keep them up. Horrid mischief would ensue were one half the world deprived of the use of them; for while avarice and ambition have a place in the heart of man, the weak will become a prey to the strong.

Thoughts on Defensive War, 1775

Disobedience

The transition from disobedience to disorder is easy and rapid.

A Friend to Rhode-Island and the Union, 1783

Disposition

It is an error very frequently committed in the world to mistake disposition for condition.

Prospects on the Rubicon, 1787

Distress

It generally happens that distress is the forerunner of benevolence; at least it serves to quicken into action that which might otherwise take a longer time to awake.

Pennsylvania Packet, October 16, 1779

Look back on any scene or subject that once gave you distress, for all of us have felt some, and you will find, that though the remembrance of the fact is not extinct in your memory, the feeling is extinct in your mind. You can remember when you had felt distress, but you cannot feel distress again, and perhaps will wonder you felt it then. It is like a shadow that loses itself by light.

Forgetfulness, 1794

Diversity

❧ ❧

That difficulties and differences will arise in communities ought always to be looked for. The opposition of interests, real or supposed; the variety of judgments; the contrariety of temper; and, in short, the whole composition of man, in his individual capacity, is tinctured with a disposition to contend.

Public Good, 1780

Doubt

❧ ❧

Doubtfulness is the opposite of belief.

Age of Reason, II, 1795

Dreams

❧ ❧

. . . I sunk insensibly into slumber. The wildest fancies in that state of *forgetfulness* always appear regular and connected; nothing is wrong in a dream, be it ever so unnatural. I am apt to think that the wisest men dream the most inconsistently. For as the judgment has nothing or very little to do in regulating the circumstances of a dream, it necessarily follows that the more powerful and creative the imagination is, the wilder it runs in that state of unrestrained invention; while those who are unable to wander out of the track of common thinking when awake, never exceed the boundaries of common nature when asleep.

The Dream Interpreted, 1775

Duty

That in which every man is interested is every man's duty to support. And any burthen which falls equally on all men, and, from which every man is to receive an equal benefit, is consistent with the most perfect ideas of liberty.

The American Crisis, 1778

A man needs no pecuniary inducement to do that to which the two-fold powers of duty and disposition naturally lead him on.

Pennsylvania Packet, July 31, 1779

Perform your own duty first, and then you will have right to make other people perform theirs.

A Friend to Rhode-Island and the Union, 1783

The duty of man is not a wilderness of turnpike gates, through which he is to pass by tickets from one to the other. It is plain and simple, and consists but of two points. His duty to God, which every man must feel; and with respect to his neighbor, to do as he would be done by.

Rights of Man, 1792

When we speak of right we ought always to unite it with the idea of duties: rights become duties by reciprocity. The right which I enjoy becomes my duty to guarantee it to another, and he to me; and those who violate the duty justly incur a forfeiture of the right.

Dissertation on First Principles of Government, 1795

Education

A nation under a well regulated government, should permit none to remain uninstructed. It is monarchical and aristocratical government only that requires ignorance for its support.

Rights of Man, II, 1792

As to the learning that any person gains from school education, it serves only, like a small capital, to put him in the way of beginning learning for himself afterwards. Every person of learning is finally his own teacher; the reason of which is, that principles, being of a distinct quality to circumstances, cannot be impressed upon the memory. Their place of mental residence is the understanding, and they are never so lasting as when they begin by conception.

Age of Reason, I, 1794

Elections

That the *elected* might never form to themselves an interest separate from the *electors*, prudence will point out the propriety of having elections often.

Common Sense, 1776

To elect and to reject, is the prerogative of a free people.

To the Citizens of the United States, 1802

An appeal to elections, decides better than an appeal to the sword.

To the Citizens of the United States, 1802

Ends

The cheat lies in putting the consequences for the cause.

The Forester's Letters, 1776

Ends and Means

It is always necessary that the means that are to accomplish any end, be equal to the accomplishment of that end, or the end cannot be accomplished.

Age of Reason, I, 1794

Enemies

Men do not change from enemies to friends by the alteration of a name.

Common Sense, 1776

To talk of friendship with those in whom our reason forbids us to have faith, and our affections wounded through a thousand pores instruct us to detest, is madness and folly.

Common Sense, 1776

It is from our enemies that we often gain excellent maxims, and are frequently surprised into reason by their mistakes.

Common Sense, 1776

Nations, like individuals, who have long been enemies, without knowing each other, or knowing why, become the better friends when they discover the errors and impositions under which they had acted.

Rights of Man, II, 1792

English Constitution

❧ ❧

The continual use of the word *Constitution* in the English Parliament shews there is none; and that the whole is merely a form of Government without a Constitution, and constituting itself with what powers it pleases. If there were a Constitution, it certainly could be referred to; and the debate on any constitutional point, would terminate by producing the Constitution. One member says, This is Constitution; another says, That is Constitution—Today it is one thing; and tomorrow, it is something else—while the maintaining the debate proves there is none. Constitution is now the cant word of Parliament, tuning itself to the ear of the Nation. Formerly it was the *universal supremacy of Parliament*—the *omnipotence of Parliament*: But, since the progress of Liberty in France, those phrases have a despotic harshness in their note; and the English Parliament have catched the fashion from the National Assembly, but without the substance, of speaking of *Constitution*.

Rights of Man, I, 1791

Enlightened Attitudes

❧ ❧

The mind once enlightened cannot again become dark. There is no possibility, neither is there any term to express the supposition by, of the mind unknowing anything it already knows.

Letter to the Abbé Raynal, 1782

Envy

❧ ❧

So unhappy is the spirit of envy, that it can be just to no merit but its own.

To the Opposers of the Bank, 1787

Equality of Man

❧ ❧

Where there are no distinctions there can be no superiority, perfect equality affords no temptation.

Common Sense, 1776

Every history of the creation, and every traditionary account, whether from the lettered or unlettered world, however they may vary in their opinion or belief of certain particulars, all agree in establishing one point, *the unity of man*; by which I mean that man is all of *one degree*, and consequently that all men are born equal, and with equal natural rights.

Rights of Man, I, 1791

Error

❧ ❧

When man have departed from the right way, it is no wonder that they stumble and fall.

Common Sense, 1776

Error like guilt is unwilling to die.

To the Opposers of the Bank, 1787

It is always better policy to leave removable errors to expose themselves, than to hazard too much in contending against them theoretically.

To George Washington, August 3, 1796

It is vain to lament an evil that is past. There is neither manhood nor policy in grief; and it often happens that an error in politics, like an error in war, admits of being turned to greater advantage than if it had not occurred.

To the People of France and the French Armies, 1797

Even Error has a claim to indulgence, if not to respect, when it is believed to be truth.

To Samuel Adams, Washington, January 1, 1803

Errors in theory are, sooner or later, accompanied with errors in practice.

Constitutions, Governments, and Charters, 1805

Europe

❧ ☙

Europe, and not England, is the parent country of America.

Common Sense, 1776

Events

❧ ☙

Providence best knows how to time her misfortunes as well as her immediate favors.

The American Crisis, 1777

Things best explain themselves by their events.

Rights of Man, I, 1791

Evils

❧ ❧

Evils, like poisons, have their uses, and there are diseases which no other remedy can reach.

The Crisis, 1778

An evil cured is better than an evil concealed and suffocated.

Pennsylvania Packet, February 16, 1779

Examples

❧ ❧

From the errors of other nations, let us learn wisdom, and lay hold of the present opportunity.

Common Sense, 1776

Expedience

❧ ❧

Expedience and right are different things.

Common Sense, 1776

Experience

❧ ❧

Experience, sad and painful experience has taught me.

The Crisis, 1778

Let us look back on the scenes we have passed, and learn from experience what is yet to be done.

The Crisis, 1783

The affairs of a nation are but unsafely trusted where the benefit of experience is wanting.

Prospects on the Rubicon, 1787

Fables

The world has been over run with fable and creeds of human invention.

To Samuel Adams, Washington, January 1, 1803

Face Saving

Considering how unwilling men are to recede from fixed opinions, and that they feel something like disgrace to being convinced, the way to obtain something is to give something.

To Robert Morris, December 7, 1782

Factions

There is too much *common sense* and independence in America to be long the dupe of any faction, foreign or domestic.

Common Sense, 1776; *To the Citizens of the United States*, 1802

Facts

Facts need but little arguments when they prove themselves.
Thoughts on Defensive War, 1775

Let our opinions be what they will, truth as to facts should be strictly adhered to.
The Forester's Letters, 1776

Fact is superior to reasoning.
Rights of Man, II, 1792

A man may often see reason, and he has too always the right, of changing his *opinion*, but this liberty does not extend to matters of fact.
Age of Reason, II, 1795

False Optimism

One broken leg is better than two, but still it is not joy.
Common Sense on George III's Speech, 1782

False Testimony

False testimony is always good against itself.
Age of Reason, II, 1795

Fame

Honest men are naturally more tender of their civil than their political fame.

The American Crisis, 1777

It is not natural that fame should wish for a rival, but the case is otherwise with me, for I do most sincerely wish there was some person in this country that could usefully and successfully attract the public attention, and leave me with a satisfied mind to the enjoyment of quiet life.

To George Washington, July 21, 1791

When a man is famous, and his name is abroad, he is made the putative father of things he never said or did.

Age of Reason, II, 1795

Farmers

The first useful class of citizens are the farmers and cultivators. These may be called citizens of the first necessity, because every thing comes originally from the earth.

To Henry Laurens, Spring 1778

The cultivator and the manufacturer are the primary means of all the wealth that exists in the world, beyond what nature spontaneously produces.

Dissertation on First Principles of Government, 1795

Farming

Every individual, high or low, is interested in the fruits of the earth; men, women, and children, of all ages and degrees, will turn out to assist the farmer, rather than a harvest should not be got in; and they will not act thus by any other property. It is the only one for which the common prayer of mankind is put up, and the only one that can never fail from the want of means. It is the interest, not of the policy, but of the existence of man, and when it ceases he must cease to be.

No other interest in a nation stands on the same united support. Commerce, manufactures, arts, sciences, and every thing else, compared with this, are supported but in parts. Their prosperity or their decay has not the same universal influence. When the valleys laugh and sing, it is not the farmer only, but all creation that rejoices. It is a prosperity that excludes all envy; and this cannot be said of any thing else.

Rights of Man, II, 1792

Fines

Fines are, of all modes of revenue, the most unsuited to the mind of a free country. When a man pays a tax, he knows the public necessity requires it, and therefore feels a pride in discharging his duty; but a fine seems an atonement for neglect of duty, and of consequence is paid with discredit, and frequently levied with severity.

The Crisis Extraordinary, 1780

First Impressions

It is but seldom that our first thoughts are truly correct.

Common Sense, 1776

It is seldom that our first thought, even upon any subject, is sufficiently just.

To the People of France and the French Armies, 1797

First Principles

When precedents fail to assist us, we must return to the first principles of things for information; and *think*, as if we were the *first men* that *thought*.

The Forester's Letters, 1776

Flattery

It is not my custom to flatter, but to serve mankind.

Common Sense on Financing the War, 1782

Folly

It is better to correct folly with wisdom, than wisdom with folly; . . . it would be much better to reject the folly entirely.

Rights of Man, II, 1792

It is surprising to what pitch of infatuation blind folly and obstinacy will carry mankind.

The American Crisis, 1777

Foolish Risks

A general is a fool and a politician is the same, who fights a battle he might avoid, and where the disasters if he is beaten far outweighs the advantages if he succeeds.

To Thomas Jefferson, January 30, 1806

Foolish Things

Wise men are astonished at foolish things.

Rights of Man, I, 1791

Fools

It is my fate to be always plagued with fools.

To the Citizens of the United States, 1802

Foppery

We pardon foppery because of its insignificance.

Dissertation on First Principles of Government, 1795

Foreign Affairs

Forms of government have nothing to do with treaties. The former are the internal police of the countries severally; the latter their external police jointly: and so long as each performs its part, we have no more right or business to know how the one or the other conducts its domestic affairs, than we have to inquire into the private concerns of a family.

Letter to the Abbé Raynal, 1782

When nations dispute, it is not so much about words as about things.

To George Washington, February 22, 1795

Foreign Opinion

It is sometimes of advantage to the people of one country, to hear what those of other countries have to say respecting it.

Rights of Man, I, 1791

Forgetfulness

Forgetfulness, is following us night and day with her opium wand, and gently touching first one, and then another, benumbs them into rest, and at last glides them away with the silence of a departing shadow. It is thus the tortured mind is restored to the calm condition of ease, and fitted for happiness.

Forgetfulness, 1794

Form

It may perhaps be said as an excuse for bad forms, that they are nothing more than forms; but this is a mistake. Forms grow out of principles, and operate to continue the principles they grow from. It is impossible to practice a bad form on any thing but a bad principle. It cannot be engrafted on a good one; and wherever the forms in any government are bad, it is a certain indication that the principles are bad also.

Rights of Man, I, 1791

So intimate is the connection between *form* and *practice*, that to adopt the one is to invite the other.

To George Washington, August 3, 1796

Forms of Government

Security being the true design and end of government, it unanswerably follows that whatever *form* thereof appears most likely to ensure it to us, with the least expense and greatest benefit, is preferable to all others.

Common Sense, 1776

The scripture institutes no particular form of government, but it enters a protest against the monarchical form; and a negation on *one* thing, where *two only* are offered, and *one* must be chosen, amounts to an affirmative on the *other*.

The Forester's Letters, 1776

The form of government best calculated for preserving liberty in time of peace, is not the best form for conducting the operations of war.

On the Affairs of Pennsylvania, 1786

If we are asked, what government is? We hold it to be nothing more than a NATIONAL ASSOCIATION, and we hold that to be the best which secures to every man his rights, and promotes the greatest quantity of happiness with the *least expense*.

Address and Declaration, 1791

Fortitude

※ ※

There is a natural firmness in some minds which cannot be unlocked by trifles, but which, when unlocked, discovers a cabinet of fortitude.

The American Crisis, 1776,
In speaking of George Washington

I have nothing to fear unless innocence and fortitude be crimes.

To James Monroe, October 1794

Foundations for Debate

※ ※

Before anything can be reasoned upon to a conclusion, certain facts, principles, or data, to reason from must be established, admitted, or denied.

Rights of Man, I, 1791

Fraud

※ ※

It is with a pious fraud as with a bad action; it begets a calamitous necessity of going on.

Age of Reason, I, 1794

Fraud once detected cannot be re-acted. To attempt it is to provoke derision, or invite destruction.

Dissertation on First Principles of Government, 1795

Freedom

Freedom hath been hunted round the globe. Asia and Africa have long expelled her. Europe regards her like a stranger, and England hath given her warning to depart. Oh, receive the fugitive, and prepare in time an asylum for mankind.

Common Sense, 1776

A freeman is a stranger no where, a slave, every where.

The Forester's Letters, 1776

Those who expect to reap the blessings of Freedom, must, like men, undergo the fatigue of supporting it.

The American Crisis, 1777

It is the nature of freedom to be free. . . . Freedom is the associate of innocence, not the companion of suspicion. She only requires to be cherished, not to be caged, and to be beloved, is, to her, to be protected.

A Serious Address to the People of Pennsylvania, 1778

Remember, that in all countries where the freedom of the poor has been taken away, in whole or in part, that the freedom of the rich lost its defence. The circle has ever continued to constrict, till lessening to a point it became absolute. Freedom must have all or none, and she must have them equally.

A Serious Address to the People of Pennsylvania, 1778

Freedom and fortune have no natural relation. They are as distinct as rest and motion.

A Serious Address to the People of Pennsylvania, 1778

Freedom is as level as water.
A Serious Address to the People of Pennsylvania, 1778

Freedom in the subject is not a diminution, as was formerly believed, of the power of government, but an increase of it.
Prospects on the Rubicon, 1787

It is impossible to conquer a nation determined to be free!
Letter to the People of France, 1792

When a whole nation acts as an army, the despot knows not the extent of the power against which he contends. New armies arise against him with the necessity of the moment. It is then that the difficulties of an invading enemy multiply . . . and he finds them at their height when he expected them to end.
Letter to the People of France, 1792

Friendship

🌿

The intimacy which is contracted in infancy, and the friendship which is formed in misfortune, are, of all others, the most lasting and unalterable.
Common Sense, 1776

A firm bargain and a right reckoning make long friends.
Common Sense, 1776

It is the fate of friendship, that where it is not accepted it is sure to offend.
Letters on the Bank, 1786

That no condition we can enjoy is an exemption from care—that some shade will mingle itself with the brightest sunshine of life—that even our affections may become the instruments of our sorrows—that the sweet felicities of home depend on good temper as well as on good sense, and that there is always something to forgive even in the nearest and dearest of our friends,—are truths which, though too obvious to be told, ought never to be forgotten.

To Kitty Nicholson Few, January 6, 1789

The idea of forsaking old friendships for new acquaintances is not agreeable.

To James Monroe, September 10, 1794

Future Generations

There never did, there never will, and there never can exist a parliament, or any description of men, or any generation of men, in any country, possessed of the right or the power of binding and controlling posterity to the *"end of time,"* or of commanding for ever how the world shall be governed, or who shall govern it: and therefore all such clauses, acts or declarations, by which the makers of them attempt to do what they have neither the right nor the power to do, nor the power to execute, are in themselves null and void. Every age and generation must be as free to act for itself, *in all cases*, as the ages and generations which preceded it. The vanity and presumption of governing beyond the grave, is the most ridiculous and insolent of all tyrannies. Man has no property in man; neither has any generation a property in the generations which are to follow.

Rights of Man, I, 1791

Every generation is and must be competent to all the purposes which its occasions require. It is the living, and not the dead, that are to be accommodated. When man ceases to be, his power and his wants cease with him.

Rights of Man, I, 1791

Every generation is equal in rights to the generations which preceded it, by the same rule that every individual is born equal in rights with his cotemporary.

Rights of Man, I, 1791

The equal rights of every generation is a fixed right in the nature of things; it belongs to the son when of age, as it belonged to the father before him.

To George Washington, August 3, 1796

Genius

An unexercised genius soon contracts a kind of mossiness, which not only checks its growth, but abates its natural vigor. Like an untenanted house it falls into decay, and frequently ruins the possessor.

The Pennsylvania Magazine, I, 1775

It would be a blessing to mankind if God would never give a genius without principle.

A Serious Address to the People of Pennsylvania, 1778

There may be genius without prostitution.

The Crisis, 1783

Judgment is a different thing from genius.

Prospects on the Rubicon, 1787

Revolutions create genius and talents; but those events do no more than bring them forward. There is existing in man, a mass of sense lying in a dormant state, and which, unless something excites it to action, will descend with him, in that condition to the grave.

Rights of Man, II, 1792

Geography

※

However strongly the passionate politics of the moment may operate, the politics that arise from geographical situation are the most
certain, and will in all cases finally prevail.

Age of Reason, I, 1794

Goals

※

The object, contended for, ought always to bear some just proportion to the expence.

Common Sense, 1776

It ought not to be, that because we cannot do every thing, that we
ought not to do what we can.

Public Good, 1780

Every object a man pursues, is, for the time, a kind of mistress to his
mind; if both are good or bad, the union is natural; but if they are in
reverse, and neither can seduce nor yet reform the other, the opposition grows into dislike, and a separation follows.

Letter to the Abbé Raynal, 1782

When men unite in agreeing that a *thing* is *good*, . . . the object is
more than half accomplished.

Rights of Man, II, 1792

It is with war as it is with law. In law, the first merits of the case become lost in the multitude of arguments; and in war they become
lost in the variety of events. New objects arise that take the lead of
all that went before, and everything assumes a new aspect.

Age of Reason, I, 1794

God

✿ ❀

Man is ever a stranger to the ways by which Providence regulates the order of things.

Letter to the People of France, 1792

The only idea man can affix to the name of God, is, that of a *first cause*, the cause of all things. And incomprehensibly difficult as it is for man to conceive what a first cause is, he arrives at the belief of it, from the tenfold greater difficulty of disbelieving it. It is difficult beyond description to conceive that space can have no end; but it is more difficult to conceive an end. It is difficult beyond the power of man to conceive an eternal duration of what we call time; but it is more impossible to conceive a time when there shall be no time. In like manner of reasoning, every thing we behold carries in itself the internal evidence that it did not make itself . . .; and it is the conviction arising from this evidence, that carries us on, as it were, by necessity, to the belief of a first cause eternally existing, of a nature totally different to any material existence we know of, and by the power of which all things exist, and this first cause man calls God.

Age of Reason, I, 1794

First, canst thou by *searching* find out God? Yes. Because, in the first place, I know I did not make myself, and yet I have existence; and by *searching* into the nature of other things, I find that no other thing could make itself; and yet millions of other things exist; therefore it is, that I know, by positive conclusion resulting from this search, that there is a power superior to all those things, and that power is God.

Age of Reason, I, 1794

Our ideas, not only of the Almightiness of the Creator, but of his wisdom and his beneficence, become enlarged in proportion as we contemplate the extent and the structure of the universe.

Age of Reason, I, 1794

It is only by the exercise of reason, that man can discover God.

Age of Reason, I, 1794

To the Almighty all things are possible.

Age of Reason, II, 1795

The Almighty is the great mechanic of the creation; the first philosopher and the original teacher of all science.

Age of Reason, II, 1795

The notion of a trinity of gods has enfeebled the belief of *one* God.

Age of Reason, II, 1795

We can know God only through his works.

Age of Reason, II, 1795

The creator of man is the creator science, and it is through that medium that man can see God, as it were, face to face.

Age of Reason, II, 1795

Do we want to contemplate His power? We see it in the immensity of the Creation. Do we want to contemplate His wisdom? We see it in the unchangeable order by which the incomprehensible WHOLE is governed. Do we want to contemplate His munificence? We see it in the abundance with which He fills the earth. Do we want to contemplate His mercy? We see it in His not withholding that abundance even from the unthankful. In fine, do we want to know what GOD is? Search not written or printed books, but the Scripture called the *creation*.

A Discourse at the Society of Theophilanthropists, 1797; To Samuel Adams, Washington, January 1, 1803; *Age of Reason*, I, 1794 (slight variation)

Let us examine this subject; it is worth examining; for if we examine it through all its cases, the result will be that the existence of a SUPERIOR CAUSE, or that which man calls GOD, will be discoverable by philosophical principles.

A Discourse at the Society of Theophilanthropists, 1797

Going the Full Course

We have at present steered with safety through a rough sea, and are bringing the ship into port, let us take care she is not shipwrecked in the harbor.

Prospects for War between Britain and France, 1778

Gold and Silver

Gold and silver are the emissions of nature: paper is the emission of art. The value of gold and silver is ascertained by the quantity which nature has made in the earth. We cannot make that quantity more or less than it is, and therefore the value being dependent upon the quantity, depends not on man. Man has no share in making gold or silver; all that his labor and ingenuity can accomplish is, to collect it from the mine, refine it for use and give it an impression, or stamp it into coin.

Dissertations on Government, 1786

Good and Bad

Male and female are the distinctions of nature, good and bad the distinctions of heaven.

Common Sense, 1776

Good Versus Bad Causes

❧ ✿

Misfortune ever separates men in a bad cause, and unites them in a good one. The former are industrious only while they are prosperous, the latter while they are distressed. The one acts from impulse, the other from contrivance; and the whole mode and progress of their conduct, and their times of rest and action, are the reverse of each other.

The Necessity of Taxation, 1782

As we have learned knowledge from misfortune, let us likewise learn it from mistake.

The Necessity of Taxation, 1782

Government

❧ ✿

Government, like dress, is the badge of lost innocence; the palaces of kings are built on the ruins of the bowers of paradise. For were the impulses of conscience clear, uniform, and irresistibly obeyed, man would need no other lawgiver; but that not being the case, he finds it necessary to surrender up a part of his property to furnish means for the protection of the rest; and this he is induced to do by the same prudence which in every other case advises him out of two evils to choose the least.

Common Sense, 1776

A government of our own is our natural right.

Common Sense, 1776

Government should always be considered as a matter of convenience, not of right.

The Forester's Letters, 1776

A faithless or arbitrary government cannot be trusted.

On the Affairs of Pennsylvania, 1786

The fundamental principles of civil government are security of our rights and persons as freemen, and security of property.

Attack on Paper Money Laws, 1786

The Government, to be of real use, should possess a complete knowledge of all the parties—all the circumstances—and all the interests of a Nation.

To the Authors of "The Republican," 1791

We hold that the moral obligation of providing for old age, helpless infancy, and poverty, is far superior to that of supplying the invented wants of courtly extravagance, ambition and intrigue.

Address and Declaration of the Friends of Universal Peace and Liberty, 1791

If we are asked, what government is? We hold it to be nothing more than a NATIONAL ASSOCIATION, and we hold that to be the best which secures to every man his rights, and promotes the greatest quantity of happiness with the *least expense*.

Address and Declaration, 1791

It is not among the least of the evils of the present existing governments in all parts of Europe, that man, considered as man, is thrown back to a vast distance from his Maker, and the artificial chasm filled up by a succession of barriers, or a sort of turnpike gates, through which he has to pass. I will quote Mr. Burke's catalogue of barriers that he has set up between man and his Maker. Putting himself in the character of a herald, he says—"We fear God—we look with *awe* to kings—with affection to parliaments—with duty to magistrates—with reverence to priests, and with respect to nobility." Mr. Burke has forgot to put in *"chivalry."* He has also forgot to put in Peter [i.e., the Pope].

The duty of man is not a wilderness of turnpike gates, through which he is to pass by tickets from one to the other. It is plain and simple, and consists but of two points. His duty to God, which every man must feel; and with respect to his neighbor, to do as he would be done by.

Rights of Man, I, 1791

111

In casting our eyes over the world, it is extremely easy to distinguish the governments which have arisen out of society, or out of the social compact, from those which have not: but to place this in a clearer light than what a single glance may afford, it will be proper to take a review of the several sources from which governments have arisen, and on which they have been founded.

They may be all comprehended under three heads. First, Superstition. Secondly, Power. Thirdly, the common interest of society, and the common *rights of man*.

The first was a government of priestcraft; the second of conquerors, and the third of reason.

Rights of Man, I, 1791

As there is but one species of man, there can be but one element of human power; and that element is man himself. Monarchy, aristocracy, and democracy, are but creatures of imagination; and a thousand such may be contrived, as well as three.

Rights of Man, I, 1791

What is government more than the management of the affairs of a Nation?

Rights of Man, I, 1791

Government is no farther necessary than to supply the few cases to which society and civilization are not conveniently competent; and instances are not wanting to show, that every thing which government can usefully add thereto, has been performed by the common consent of society, without government.

Rights of Man, II, 1792

Government is nothing more than a national association acting on the principles of society.

Rights of Man, II, 1792

The strength of government does not consist in any thing *within* itself, but in the attachment of a nation, and the interest which the people feel in supporting it. When this is lost, government is but a child in power; and though . . . it may harass individuals for a while, it but facilitates its own fall.

Rights of Man, II, 1792

Government is not a trade which any man or body of men has a right to set up and exercise for his own emolument, but is altogether a trust, in right of those by whom that trust is delegated, and by whom it is always resumeable. It has of itself no rights; they are altogether duties.

Rights of Man, II, 1792

Government is nothing more than a national association; and the object of this association is the good of all, as well individually as collectively.

Rights of Man, II, 1792

When it shall be said in any country in the world, my poor are happy, neither ignorance nor distress is to be found among them; my jails are empty of prisoners, my streets of beggars; the aged are not in want, the taxes are not oppressive; the rational world is my friend, because I am the friend of its happiness: when these things can be said, then may that country boast its constitution and its government.

Rights of Man, II, 1792

It is time that nations should be rational, and not be governed like animals, for the pleasure of their riders.

Rights of Man, II, 1792

Government Authority

The necessity of always fitting our internal police to the circumstances of the times we live in, is something so strikingly obvious that no sufficient objection can be made against it. The safety of all societies depend upon it; and where this point is not attended to, the consequence will either be a general languor or a tumult. The encouragement and protection of the good subjects of any State, and the suppression and punishment of bad ones, are the principal objects for which all authority is instituted, and the line in which it ought to operate.

The American Crisis, 1777

The governing rule of *right* and mutual good must in all public cases finally preside.

Public Good, 1780

Government Forms

It may perhaps be said as an excuse for bad forms, that they are nothing more than forms; but this is a mistake. Forms grow out of principles, and operate to continue the principles they grow from. It is impossible to practice a bad form on any thing but a bad principle. It cannot be ingrafted on a good one; and wherever the forms in any government are bad, it is a certain indication that the principles are bad also.

Rights of Man, I, 1791

Great Objects

Great objects inspire great thoughts; great munificence excites great gratitude.

Age of Reason, II, 1795

Greatness

Greatness is nothing where it is not seen.

A Serious Address to the People of Pennsylvania, 1778

Grief

All grief, like all things else, will yield to the obliterating power of time.

Forgetfulness, 1794

It is vain to lament an evil that is past. There is neither manhood nor policy in grief.

To the People of France and the French Armies, 1797

Guilt of Government

The guilt of government is the crime of a whole country.

To the Earl of Shelburne, 1782

Gullibility

We are not now, Sir, to be led away by the jingle of a phrase.

The Forester's Letters, 1776

The more unnatural any thing is, the more is it capable of becoming the object of dismal admiration.

Age of Reason, I, 1794

Habit

✤ ✤

A long habit of not thinking a thing *wrong*, gives it a superficial appearance of being *right*, and raises at first a formidable outcry in defence of custom.

Common Sense, 1776

Half-Way Measures

✤ ✤

The worst of all policy is that of doing things by halves. Penny-wise and pound foolish has been the ruin of thousands.

The American Crisis, 1778

Doing things by halves will answer no purpose but that of increasing her expenses in the end.

To William Short, June 24 and 25, 1790

When it becomes necessary to do a thing, the whole heart and soul should go into the measure, or not attempt it.

Rights of Man, I, 1791

Happiness

✤ ✤

For the first and great question, and that which involves every other in it, and from which every other will flow, is happiness.

The Forester's Letters, 1776

Whatever the apparent cause of any riots may be, the real one is always want of happiness.

Rights of Man, II, 1792

Whatever the form or constitution of government may be, it ought to have no other object than the *general* happiness.

Rights of Man, II, 1792

Hardships

✿

It is a long lane that has no turning.

The Crisis, 1778

Harmony

✿

Harmony and friendship is nevertheless the happiest condition a country can be blessed with.

The American Crisis, 1777

The harmony of the whole is composed of the harmony of its parts; and in proportion as any of them is disordered, the collective force will be weakened, and the general tranquility disturbed.

Serious Address to the People of Pennsylvania, 1778

Hasty Judgments

✿

The misfortune is, that partly from the pressing necessity of some instant things, and partly from the impatience of our own tempers, we are frequently in such a hurry to make out the meaning of every thing as fast as it happens, that we thereby never truly understand it; and not only start new difficulties to ourselves by so doing, but, as it were, embarrass Providence in her good design.

The American Crisis, 1777

Health

※ ⚘

I have yet, I believe, some years in store, for I have a good state of health and a happy mind, and I take care of both by nourishing the first with temperance and the latter with abundance. This, I believe, you will allow to be the true philosophy of life.

To Samuel Adams, Washington, January 1, 1803

Heaven

※ ⚘

The key of heaven is not in the keeping of any sect, nor ought the road to it be obstructed by any.

To Samuel Adams, Washington, January 1, 1803

Hell

※ ⚘

If we believe the power of hell to be limited, we must likewise believe that their agents are under some providential control.

The American Crisis, 1776

The Hereafter

※ ⚘

I believe in one God, and no more; and I hope for happiness beyond this life.

Age of Reason, I, 1794

I trouble not myself about the manner of future existence. I content myself with believing, even to positive conviction, that the power that gave me existence is able to continue it, in any form and manner he pleases, either with or without this body; and it appears more probable to me that I shall continue to exist hereafter, than that I should have had existence, as I now have, before that existence began.

Age of Reason, I, 1794

The probability that we *may be* called to account hereafter, will, to reflecting minds, have the influence of belief; for it is not our belief or our disbelief, that can make or unmake the fact. As this is the state we are in, and which it is proper we should be in as free agents, it is the fool only, and not the philosopher, nor even the prudent man, that will live as if there were no God.

Age of Reason, II, 1795

As a matter of choice, as well as of hope, I had rather have a better body and a more convenient form, than the present.

Age of Reason, II, 1795

But all other arguments apart, the *consciousness of existence* is the only conceivable idea we can have of another life, and the continuance of that consciousness is immortality. The consciousness of existence, or of knowing that we exist, is not necessarily confined to the same form, nor to the same matter, even in this life. We have not in all cases the same form, nor in any case the same matter, that composed our bodies twenty or thirty years ago, and yet we are conscious of being the same persons. Even legs and arms, which make up almost half the human frame, are not necessary to the consciousness of existence. These may be lost or taken away, and the full consciousness of existence remain, and were their place supplied by wings, or other appendages, we cannot conceive that it could alter our consciousness of existence. In short, we know not how much, or rather how little, of our composition it is, and how exquisitely fine that little is, that creates in us this consciousness of existence, and all beyond that is like the pulp of a peach, distinct and separate from the vegetative speck in the kernel.

Age of Reason, II, 1795

I consider myself in the hands of my Creator, and that He will dispose of me after this life consistently with His justice and goodness. I leave all these matters to Him, as my Creator and friend, and I hold it to be presumption in man to make an article of faith as to what the Creator will do with us hereafter. I do not believe because a man and a woman make a child that it imposes on the Creator the unavoidable obligation of keeping the being so made in eternal existence hereafter. It is in His power to do so, or not to do so, and it is not in our power to decide which He will do.

Examination of the Prophecies, 1807

My own opinion is, that those whose lives have been spent in doing good, and endeavoring to make their fellow-mortals happy, for this is the only way in which we can serve God, will be happy hereafter; and that the very wicked will meet with some punishment. But those who are neither good nor bad, or are too insignificant for notice, will be dropped entirely.

Examination of the Prophecies, 1807

Hereditary Government

❧ ❧

For all men being originally equals, no *one* by *birth* could have a right to set up his own family in perpetual preference to all others forever, and though himself might deserve *some* decent degree of honors of his cotemporaries, yet his descendants might be far too unworthy to inherit them. One of the strongest *natural* proofs of the folly of hereditary right in kings, is that nature disapproves it, otherwise she would not so frequently turn it into ridicule by giving mankind an *ass for a lion*.

Common Sense, 1776

As the exercise of Government requires talents and abilities, and as talents and abilities cannot have hereditary descent, it is evident that hereditary succession requires a belief from man, to which his reason cannot subscribe, and which can only be established upon his ignorance; and the more ignorant any country is, the better it is fitted for this species of Government.

Rights of Man, I, 1791

All hereditary government is in its nature tyranny.

Rights of Man, II, 1792

To inherit a government, is to inherit the people, as if they were flocks and herds.

Rights of Man, II, 1792

Hereditary succession is a burlesque upon monarchy. It puts it in the most ridiculous light, by presenting it as an office which any child or idiot may fill.

Rights of Man, II, 1792

A government calling itself free, with an hereditary office, is like a thorn in the flesh, that produces a fermentation which endeavors to discharge it.

Rights of Man, II, 1792

There is not a problem in Euclid more mathematically true than that hereditary government has not a right to exist.

Dissertation on First Principles of Government, 1795

Hints

I only presume to offer hints, not plans.

Common Sense, 1776

History

In the progress of politics, as in the common occurrences of life, we are not only apt to forget the ground we have travelled over, but frequently neglect to gather up experience as we go. We expend, if I may so say, the knowledge of every day on the circumstances that produce it, and journey on in search of new matter and new refinements: But as it is pleasant, and sometimes useful, to look back, even to the first periods of infancy, and trace the turns and windings through which we have passed, so we may likewise derive many advantages by halting a while in our political career, and taking a review of the wondrous complicated labyrinth of little more than yesterday.

The American Crisis, 1777

A too great inattention to past occurrences retards and bewilders our judgment in every thing; while, on the contrary, by comparing what is past with what is present, we frequently hit on the true character of both, and become wise with very little trouble. It is a kind of countermarch, by which we get into the rear of Time, and mark the movements and meaning of things as we make our return.

The American Crisis, 1777

To unite time with circumstance, is a material nicety in history; the want of which frequently throws it into endless confusion and mistake, occasions a total separation between causes and consequences and connects them with others they are not immediately, and sometimes not at all, related to.

Letter to the Abbé Raynal, 1782

Every thing must have had a beginning, and the fog of time and antiquity should be penetrated to discover it.

Rights of Man, I, 1791

Every thing which passes in the world becomes matter for history.

Rights of Man, I, 1791

It is not the antiquity of a tale that is any evidence of its truth, on the contrary it is a symptom of its being fabulous; for the more ancient any history pretends to be, the more it has the resemblance of fable.

Age of Reason, II, 1795

Honesty

Of more worth is one honest man to society and in the sight of God, than all the crowned ruffians that ever lived.

Common Sense, 1776

He who dares not offend cannot be honest.

The Forester's Letters, 1776

Learn to be an honest man, and then thou wilt not be thus exposed.

The Forester's Letters, 1776

Nothing can hurt us but want of honesty.

Pennsylvania Packet, April 13, 1779

A government or an administration, who means and acts honestly, has nothing to fear, and consequently has nothing to conceal.

Common Sense on Financing the War, 1782

Hopeless Situations

New schemes, like new medicines, have administered fresh hopes and prolonged the disease instead of curing it.

The Crisis, 1780

Human Beings

As a matter of choice, as well as of hope, I had rather have a better body and a more convenient form, than the present. Every animal in the creation excels us in something. The winged insects, without mentioning doves or eagles, can pass over more space, and with greater ease, in a few minutes, than man can in an hour. The glide of the smallest fish, in proportion to its bulk, exceeds us in motion almost beyond comparison, and without weariness. Even the sluggish snail can ascend from the bottom of a dungeon, where man by the want of that ability would perish, and a spider can launch itself from the top as a playful amusement.

Age of Reason, II, 1795

Human Nature

Human nature is not of itself vicious.

Rights of Man, II, 1792

Humanity

It is always fortunate when the interests of Government and that of humanity act unitedly.

To Thomas Jefferson, January 25, 1805

Hypocrisy

Like antiquated virgins they see not the havoc deformity hath made upon them, but pleasantly mistaking wrinkles for dimples, conceit themselves yet lovely, and wonder at the stupid world for not admiring them.

The American Crisis, 1777

It is necessary to the happiness of man, that he be mentally faithful to himself. Infidelity does not consist in believing, or in disbelieving: it consists in professing to believe what he does not believe.

Age of Reason, I, 1794

It is natural that hypocrisy should act the reverse of what it preaches.

Age of Reason, II, 1795

It is impossible to be a hypocrite and to be brave at the same instant.

To the People of France and the French Armies, 1797

There is more of hypocrisy than bigotry in America.

To Thomas Jefferson, January 25, 1805

The prejudice of unfounded belief, often degenerates into the prejudice of custom, and becomes at last rank hypocrisy. When men, from custom or fashion or any worldly motive, profess or pretend to believe what they do not believe, nor can give any reason for believing, they unship the helm of their morality, and being no longer honest to their own minds they feel no moral difficulty in being unjust to others.

Examination of the Prophecies, 1807

Ideas

❧ ❧

Let but a single idea begin and a thousand will soon follow.

Dissertation on First Principles of Government, 1795

Ignorance

❧ ❧

Where information is withheld, ignorance becomes a reasonable excuse. . . . They see not, therefore they feel not.

The Crisis, 1778

Where knowledge is a duty, ignorance is a crime.

Public Good, 1780; *Dissertations on Government*, 1786; *To the People of France and the French Armies*, 1797

Ignorance is of a peculiar nature; once dispelled, it is impossible to re-establish it. It is not originally a thing of itself, but is only the absence of knowledge; and though man may be *kept* ignorant, he cannot be *made* ignorant.

Rights of Man, I, 1791

Ignorance is his best excuse.

To George Washington, August 3, 1796

Ill Opinion

❧ ❧

No man asks another to act the villain unless he believes him to be inclined to be one. No man attempts to seduce a truly modest woman. It is the supposed looseness of her mind that starts the thought of seduction, and he who offers it calls her a prostitute.

The Crisis, 1782

Imagination

❧ ❧

Imagination supplies all deficiencies.

Age of Reason, II, 1795

If there is any faculty in mental man that never sleeps it is that volatile thing the imagination. The case is different with the judgment and memory. The sedate and sober constitution of the judgment easily disposes it to rest; and as to the memory, it records in silence and is active only when it is called upon.

An Essay on Dreams, 1802

Imitation

❧ ❧

Everything that deserves imitation is sure to be imitated.

Answers to Four Questions on Legislative and Executive Powers, 1791

Imitation is naturally progressive, and is rapidly so in matters that are vicious.

To George Washington, August 3, 1796

Impetuosity

※ ⁂

There appears a uniformity in all the works of nature, from individual animals up to nations. The smaller animals are always the most fretful, passionate and insulting. They mistake temper for strength, and often fall a sacrifice to vexatious impetuosity, while larger ones go calmly on, and require repeated provocations to incense them.

Prospects on the Rubicon, 1787

Improvement

※ ⁂

We live to improve, or we live in vain.

Address and Declaration, 1791

Inertia

※ ⁂

The probability is always greater against a thing beginning, than of proceeding after it has begun.

Rights of Man, II, 1792

Infidelity

※ ⁂

Infidelity does not consist in believing, or in disbelieving: it consists in professing to believe what he does not believe.

Age of Reason, I, 1794

Ingenuity

It seems to be a defect, connected with ingenuity, that it often employs itself more in matters of curiosity, than usefulness. . . . Whether this be a crime, or only a caprice of humanity, I am not inquiring into.

Letter to the Abbé Raynal, 1782

Ingratitude

It is not every man whose mind is strong enough to bear up against ingratitude.

Letter to Citizen Danton, May 6, 1793

The icy heart of ingratitude, in whatever man it be placed, has neither feeling nor sense of honor.

To the Citizens of the United States, 1802

Injuries

There are injuries which nature cannot forgive; she would cease to be nature if she did.

Common Sense, 1776

Insensitivity

※ ※

Enjoy your insensibility of feeling and reflecting. It is the prerogative of animals.

The American Crisis, 1778

Insinuating Lies

※ ※

An insinuation, which a man who makes it does not believe himself, is equal to lying. It is the cowardice of lying. It unites the barest part of that vice with the meanest of all others. An open liar is a highwayman in his profession, but an insinuating liar is a thief skulking in the night.

To the Opposers of the Bank, 1787

Insurrections

※ ※

It will sometimes happen that the minority are right, and the majority are wrong, but as soon as experience proves this to be the case, the minority will increase to a majority, and the error will reform itself by the tranquil operation of freedom of opinion and equality of rights. Nothing, therefore, can justify an insurrection, neither can it ever be necessary where rights are equal and opinions free.

Dissertation on First Principles of Government, 1795

Integrity

❧ ☙

The proud integrity of conscious rectitude fears no reproach.

Letters to Morgan Lewis, 1807

Intelligence

❧ ☙

Experience, in all ages, and in all countries, has demonstrated, that it is impossible to control Nature in her distribution of mental powers. She gives them as she pleases. Whatever is the rule by which she, apparently to us, scatters them among mankind, that rule remains a secret to man. It would be as ridiculous to attempt to fix the hereditaryship of human beauty, as of wisdom. Whatever wisdom constituently is, it is like a seedless plant; it may be reared when it appears, but it cannot be voluntarily produced. There is always a sufficiency somewhere in the general mass of society for all purposes; but with respect to the parts of society, it is continually changing its place. It rises in one today, in another tomorrow, and has most probably visited in rotation every family of the earth, and again withdrawn.

Rights of Man, II, 1792

Interest

❧ ☙

Interest and Time have an amazing influence over the understanding of mankind, and reconcile them to almost every species of absurdity and injustice.

Four Letters on Interesting Subjects, 1776

All the world are moved by interest, and it affords them nothing to boast of.

The Crisis, 1782

Mankind, as it appears to me, are always ripe enough to understand their true interest, provided it be presented clearly to their understanding, and that in a manner not to create suspicion by any thing like self-design, nor offend by assuming too much.

Rights of Man, II, 1792

Common interest produces common security.

Rights of Man, II, 1792

Invading Armies

There it was that the enemy, by beginning to conquer, put himself in a condition of being conquered. His first victories prepared him for defeat. He advanced till he could not retreat, and found himself in the midst of a nation of armies.

Letter to the People of France, 1792

Irrational Expressions

The expressions be pleasantly arranged, yet when examined they appear idle and ambiguous; and it will always happen, that the nicest construction that words are capable of, when applied to the description of some thing which either cannot exist, or is too incomprehensible to be within the compass of description, will be words of sound only, and though they may amuse the ear, they cannot inform the mind.

Common Sense, 1776

Irrationality

❧ ❧

To argue with a man who has renounced the use and authority of reason, and whose philosophy consists in holding humanity in contempt, is like administering medicine to the dead, or endeavoring to convert an Atheist by scripture.

The American Crisis, 1778

Irreconcilable Disputes

❧ ❧

Questions, which when determined, cannot be executed, serve only to show the folly of dispute and the weakness of disputants.

The Crisis, 1780

Jargon

❧ ❧

Every art and science has some point, or alphabet, at which the study of that art or science begins, and by the assistance of which the progress is facilitated.

Dissertation on First Principles of Government, 1795

Jesus

❧ ❧

He was a virtuous and an amiable man. The morality that he preached and practiced was of the most benevolent kind.

Age of Reason, I, 1794

He was a Jew by birth and by profession; and he was the son of God in like manner that every other person is; for the Creator is the Father of All.

Age of Reason, I, 1794

Jesus Christ founded no new system. He called men to the practice of moral virtues, and the belief of one God. The great trait in his character is philanthropy.

Age of Reason, I, 1794

Judgment

Judgment is a different thing from genius.

Prospects on the Rubicon, 1787

The sedate and sober constitution of the judgment easily disposes it to rest.

An Essay on Dreams, 1802

Jury Trial

All men are Republicans by nature and Royalists only by fashion. And this is fully proved by that passionate adoration, which all men show to that great and almost only remaining bulwark of natural rights, *trial by juries*, which is founded on a pure Republican basis. Here the power of Kings is shut out. No Royal negative can enter this Court. The Jury, which is here, supreme, is a *Republic*, a body of *Judges chosen from among the people*.

The Forester's Letters, 1776

Justice

We are never in a proper condition of doing justice to others, while we continue under the influence of some leading partiality, so neither are we capable of doing it to ourselves while we remain fettered by any obstinate prejudice.

Common Sense, 1776

But let them have regard to justice, and pay some attention to the plain doctrine of reason. Where these are wanting, the sacred cause of truth applauds our anger, and dignifies it with the name of Virtue.

The Forester's Letters, 1776

There is a kind of bastard generosity, which, by being extended to all men, is as fatal to society, on one hand, as the want of true generosity is on the other. A lax manner of administering justice, falsely termed moderation, has a tendency both to dispirit public virtue and promote the growth of public evils.

The American Crisis, 1777

When one villain is suffered to escape, it encourages another to proceed, either from a hope of escaping likewise, or an apprehension that we dare not punish.

The American Crisis, 1777

Justice is one uniform attribute, which acting in the man or in the multitude, is always the same, and produces the same consequence.

A Serious Address to the People of Pennsylvania, 1778

Justice is due, even to an enemy.

Common Sense on George III's Speech, 1782

How easy is it to abuse truth and language, when men, by habitual wickedness, have learned to set justice at defiance.

Common Sense on George III's Speech, 1782

Private justice is undoubtedly due to all men, and where that fails, public justice can have but a slender foundation.

Philadelphia *Freeman's Journal*, May 1, 1782

With respect to justice, it ought not to be left to the choice of detached individuals, whether they will do justice or not.

Agrarian Justice, 1797

Justness

❧ ⚘

The justness of their cause was a continual source of consolation.

The Crisis, 1780

To be free is a happiness—but to be JUST is an honor, if that can be called an honor which is only a duty.

A Friend to Rhode-Island and the Union, 1783

The great mass of the People are invariably just, both in their intentions, and in their object; but the true method of accomplishing that effect, does not always show itself in the first instance.

Speech to the French National Convention, January 15, 1793

Knowledge

❧ ⚘

Where knowledge is a duty, ignorance is a crime.

Public Good, 1780; *Dissertations on Government*, 1786;
To the People of France and the French Armies, 1797

Ignorance is of a peculiar nature: once dispelled, it is impossible to reestablish it. It is not originally a thing of itself, but is only the absence of knowledge; and though man may by *kept* ignorant, he cannot be *made* ignorant. The mind, in discovering truth, acts in the same manner as it acts through the eye in discovering objects; when once any object has been seen, it is impossible to put the mind back to the same condition it was in before it saw it. . . . The means must be an obliteration of knowledge; and it has never yet been discovered, how to make man *unknow* his knowledge, or *unthink* his thoughts.

Rights of Man, I, 1791

Lack of Follow-Through

To spare now, would be the height of extravagance, and to consult present ease, would sacrifice it, perhaps forever.

The Crisis, 1780

Land

Lands are the real riches of all the habitable world and the natural funds of America.

Public Good, 1780

Land is the free gift of the Creator in common to the human race.

Agrarian Justice, 1797

Language

The expressions be pleasantly arranged, yet when examined they appear idle and ambiguous; and it will always happen, that the nicest construction that words are capable of, when applied to the description of some thing which either cannot exist, or is too incomprehensible to be within the compass of description, will be words of sound only, and though they may amuse the ear, they cannot inform the mind.

Common Sense, 1776

There are cases which cannot be overdone by language.

The American Crisis, 1776

Plain language may perhaps sound uncouthly to an ear vitiated by courtly refinements; but words were made for use, and the fault lies in deserving them, or the abuse in applying them unfairly.

The American Crisis, 1777

We sometimes experience sensations to which language is not equal. The conception is too bulky to be born alive, and in the torture of thinking we stand dumb. Our feelings imprisoned by their magnitude, find no way out, and, in the struggle of expression, every finger tries to be a tongue. The machinery of the body seems too little for the mind and we look about for helps to show our thoughts by.

The Crisis, 1782

I have often observed that by lending words for my thoughts I understand my thoughts the better. Thoughts are a kind of mental smoke, which require words to illuminate them.

To Benjamin Franklin, December 31, 1785

It is necessary to affix right ideas to words.

Age of Reason, I, 1794

Human language is local and changeable.

Age of Reason, I, 1794

Law of Nations

❧⸙

No going to law with nations; cannon are the barristers of Crowns; and the sword, not of justice, but of war, decides the suit.

Common Sense, 1776

Whereas the law of nations is in theory the law of treaties compounded with customary usage, and in practice just what they can get and keep till it be taken from them. It is a term without any regular defined meaning, and as in some instances we have invented the thing first and given the name afterwards, so in this we have invented the name and the thing is yet to be made.

Peace, and the Newfoundland Fisheries, 1779

Laws

☙ ❧

In America THE LAW IS KING. For as in absolute governments the King is law, so in free countries the law *ought* to be King; and there ought to be no other.

Common Sense, 1776

It is not enough to constitute a good government; it is equally indispensable to adopt such methods as may assure the permanency of a good government.

Answers to Four Questions on Legislative and Executive Powers, 1791

I have always held it an opinion (making it also my practice) that it is better to obey a bad law, making use at the same time of every argument to show its errors and procure its repeal, than forcibly to violate it; because the precedent of breaking a bad law might weaken the force, and lead to a discretionary violation, of those which are good.

Rights of Man, II, 1792

The laws which common usage ordains, have a greater influence than the laws of government.

Rights of Man, II, 1792

All the great laws of society are laws of nature.

Rights of Man, II, 1792

The government of a free country, properly speaking, is not in the persons, but in the laws.

Rights of Man, II, 1792

Laws difficult to be executed cannot be generally good.

Rights of Man, II, 1792

We laugh at individuals for the silly difficulties they make to themselves, without perceiving, that the greatest of all ridiculous things are acted in governments.

Rights of Man, II, 1792

A law not repealed continues in force, not because it cannot be repealed, but because it is not repealed, and the non-repealing passes for consent.

Rights of Man, II, 1792

The preservation of liberty depends on obedience to the law, which is the expression of the general will. Anything that is not prohibited by the law cannot be forbidden, and no one can be constrained to do that which the law does not ordain.

Plan of a Declaration of Rights, 1792

The law should be equal for all, whether it rewards or punishes, whether it protects or restrains.

Plan of a Declaration of Rights, 1792

Lawyers

It would be a blessing to mankind if God would never give a genius without principle; and in like manner would be a happiness to society if none but honest men would be suffered to be lawyers. The wretch who will write on any subject for bread, or in any service for pay, and he who will plead in *any case* for a *fee*, stands equally in rank with the prostitute who lets out her person.

A Serious Address to the People of Pennsylvania, 1778

Lawyers and a Gentleman are characters but seldom in conjunction. When they meet the union is highly valuable, and the character truly respectable.

A Serious Address to the People of Pennsylvania, 1778

Leadership

❦

If those to whom power is delegated do well, they will be respected; if not, they will be despised.

Rights of Man, I, 1791

Legislative Tyranny

❦

At the commencement of the revolution, it was supposed that what is called the executive part of government was the only dangerous part; but we now see that quite as much mischief, if not more, may be done, and as much arbitrary conduct acted, by a legislature.

On the Affairs of Pennsylvania, 1786

Liberty

❦

Though the flame of liberty may sometimes cease to shine, the coal never can expire.

The American Crisis, 1776

The felicity which liberty insures us is transformed into virtue when we communicate its enjoyment to others.

Answers to Four Questions on Legislative and Executive Powers, 1791

Liberty cannot be purchased by a wish.

Letter to the People of France, 1792

Liberty is the power to do everything that does not interfere with the rights of others: thus, the exercise of the natural rights of every individual has no limits save those that assure to other members of society the enjoyment of the same rights.

Plan of a Declaration of Rights, 1792

He that would make his own liberty secure must guard even his enemy from oppression; for if he violates this duty, he establishes a precedent that will reach to himself.

Dissertation on First Principles of Government, 1795

Liberty and Humanity

✤

Liberty and humanity have ever been the words that best expressed my thoughts, and it is my conviction that the union of these two principles, in all cases, tends more than anything also to insure the grandeur of a nation.

Shall Louis XVI Be Respited?, 1793

My language has always been that of liberty *and* humanity, and I know that nothing so exalts a nation as the union of these two principles, under all circumstances.

Speech to the French National Convention, January 19, 1793

Liberty of the Press

❧ ☙

Nothing is more common with printers, especially of Newspapers, than the continual cry of the *liberty of the press*, as if because they are Printers they are to have more privileges than other people.

Liberty of the Press, 1806

The press, which is a tongue to the eye, was then put exactly in the case of the human tongue. A man does not ask liberty before hand to say something he has a mind to say, but he becomes answerable for the atrocities he may utter. In like manner, if a man makes the press utter atrocious things he becomes as answerable for them as if he had uttered them by word of mouth.

Liberty of the Press, 1806

Lies

❧ ☙

A continual circulation of lies among those who are not much in the way of hearing them contradicted, will in time pass for truth; and the crime lies not in the believer but the inventor.

The American Crisis, 1777

An insinuation, which a man who makes it does not believe himself, is equal to lying. It is the cowardice of lying. It unites the barest part of that vice with the meanest of all others. An open liar is a highwayman in his profession, but an insinuating liar is a thief skulking in the night.

To the Opposers of the Bank, 1787

It is an easy thing to tell a lie, but it is difficult to support the lie after it is told.

Age of Reason, II, 1795

When anything is attempted to be supported by lying, it is presumptive evidence that the thing so supported is a lie also. The stock on which a lie can be engrafted must be of the same species as the graft.

To the Citizens of the United States, 1802

Love

❧

Divided love is never happy.

Age of Reason, II, 1795

'Tis that delight some transport we can feel
Which painters cannot paint, nor words reveal
Nor any art we know of can conceal

What Is Love?, 1800

The Love of the People

❧

He that is wise will reflect, that the safest asylum, especially in times of general convulsion when no settled form of government prevails, is *the love of the people*. All property is safe under their protection.

The Forester's Letters, 1776

Loyalty of Immigrants

❧

Men soon become attached to the soil they live upon, and incorporated with the prosperity of the place: and it signifies but little what opinions they come over with, for time, interest, and new connections will render them obsolete, and the next generation know nothing of them.

Letter to the Abbé Raynal, 1782

Luxuries

❧

When taxes are proposed, the country is amused by the plausible language of taxing luxuries. One thing is called a luxury at one time, and something else at another; but the real luxury does not consist in the article, but in the means of procuring it.

Rights of Man, II, 1792

Magazines

❧

A Magazine when properly conducted, is the nursery of genius; and by constantly accumulating new matter, becomes a kind of market for wit and utility.

The Pennsylvania Magazine, I, 1775

I consider a Magazine as a kind of bee-hive, which both allures the swarm, and provides room to store their sweets. Its division into cells gives every bee a province of its own; and though they all produce honey, yet perhaps they differ in their taste for flowers, and extract with greater dexterity from one than from another. *Thus* we are not all *philosophers*, all *artists*, nor all *poets*.

The Pennsylvania Magazine, I, 1775

Majority Rule

※ ♪

No man is a true republican, or worthy of the name, that will not give up his single voice to that of the public: his private opinion he may retain; it is obedience only that is his duty.

Four Letters on Interesting Subjects, 1776

The sense of the majority is the governing sense.

A Serious Address to the People of Pennsylvania, 1778

It is always the interest of a far greater number of people in a nation to have things right, than to let them remain wrong; and when public matters are open to debate, and the public judgment free, it will not decide wrong, unless it decides too hastily.

Rights of Man, II, 1792

In all matters of opinion, the social compact, or the principle by which society is held together, requires that the majority of opinions becomes the rule for the whole, and that the minority yields practical obedience thereto.

Dissertation on First Principles of Government, 1795

Man at the Age of Fifty

※ ♪

At fifty, though the mental faculties of man are in full vigor, and his judgment better than at any preceding date, the bodily powers for laborious life are on the decline. He cannot bear the same quantity of fatigue as at an earlier period. He begins to earn less, and is less capable of enduring wind and weather; and in those more retired employments where much sight is required, he fails apace, and sees himself, like an old horse, beginning to be turned adrift.

Rights of Man, II, 1792

Manners

✿

The domestic tranquillity of a nation, depends greatly, on the *chastity* of what may properly be called *national manners.*

Common Sense, 1776

Marriage

✿

Though I appear a sort of wanderer, the married state has not a sincerer friend than I am. It is the harbor of human life, and is, with respect to the things of this world, what the next world is to this. It is home; and that one word conveys more than any other word can express. For a few years we may glide along the tide of youthful single life and be wonderfully delighted; but it is a tide that flows but once, and what is still worse, it ebbs faster than it flows, and leaves many a hapless voyager aground. I am one, you see, that have experienced the fate I am describing.

To Kitty Nicholson Few, January 6, 1789

Marriage of Female Friends

✿

When I see my female friends drop off by matrimony I am sensible of something that affects me like a loss in spite of all the appearances of joy: I cannot help mixing the sincere compliment of regret with that of congratulation. It appears as if I had outlived or lost a friend. It seems to me as if the original was no more, and that which she is changed to forsakes the circle and forgets the scenes of former society. Felicities are cares superior to those she formerly cared for, create to her a new landscape of life that excludes the little friendships of the past. It is not every lady's mind that is sufficiently capacious to prevent those greater objects crowding out the less, or that can spare a thought to former friendships after she has given her hand and heart to the man who loves her.

To Kitty Nicholson Few, January 6, 1789

Meanness

🌿 🌿

Mankind are not universally agreed in their determination of right and wrong; but there are certain actions which the consent of all nations and individuals hath branded with the unchangeable name of MEANNESS.

The American Crisis, 1778

Meanness hath neither alliance nor apology.

The American Crisis, 1778

There is something in meanness which excites a species of resentment that never subsides.

The American Crisis, 1778

Mechanics

🌿 🌿

Mechanics is no other than the principles of science applied practically.

Age of Reason, I, 1794

Memory

❧ ❧

Were a man to be totally deprived of memory, he would be incapable of forming any just opinion; every thing about him would seem a chaos; he would have even his own history to ask from every one; and by not knowing how the world went on in his absence, he would be at a loss to know how it ought to go on when he recovered, or rather, returned to it again.

The American Crisis, 1777

As to the memory, it records in silence and is active only when it is called upon.

An Essay on Dreams, 1802

Mercy

❧ ❧

It is the madness of folly to expect mercy from those who have refused to do justice.

The American Crisis, 1776

Method

❧ ❧

It is only by reducing complicated things to method and orderly connection that they can be understood with advantage, or pursued with success.

Common Sense on Financing the War, 1782

I love method, because I see and am convinced of its beauty and advantage. It is that which makes all business easy and understood, and without which every thing becomes embarrassed and difficult.

Common Sense on Financing the War, 1782

It is not all the ardor which the love of liberty can inspire, nor the utmost fortitude which the most heroic virtue can create, that will of themselves make us successful conquerors. We must come down to order, system and method, and go through the cool and judicious, as well as the animating and elevated parts of patriotism.

The Necessity of Taxation, 1782

Method is to natural power, what slight is to human strength, without strength, without which a giant would lose his labor, and a country waste its force.

The Necessity of Taxation, 1782

Military Bearing

❧ ☙

Some men have naturally a military turn, and can brave hardships and the risk of life with a cheerful face; others have not, no slavery appears to them so great as the fatigue of arms, and no terror so powerful as that of personal danger: What can we say? We cannot alter nature, neither ought we to punish the son because the father begot him in a cowardly mood. However, I believe most men have more courage than they know of, and that a little at first is enough to begin with.

The American Crisis, 1777

Military Command

A change in Generals, like a change of physicians, served only to keep the flattery alive, and furnish new pretenses for new extravagance.

The Crisis, 1780

Mischief

Mischief is easier begun than ended.

Rights of Man, I, 1791

There is not a worse character in life than that of a mischief-making blackhearted man. It is a disposition that leads to every thing that disturbs the peace of society. It works under ground like a mole, and having thrown up its little mole-hills of dirt, blows them with its pestiferous breath into mountains.

A Spark from the Altar of '76, 1805

That inability to do mischief is the best security against mischief.

To Thomas Jefferson, January 30, 1806

Misers

Can any thing be a greater inducement to a miserly man, than the hope of making his mammon safe?

The American Crisis, 1777

Misery

❧

Are there not miseries enough in the world, too difficult to be encountered and too pointed to be borne, without studying to enlarge the list and arming it with new destruction? Is life so very long that it is necessary, nay even a duty, to shake the sand and hasten out the period of duration? Is the path so elegantly smooth, so decked on every side and carpeted with joys, that wretchedness is wanting to enrich it as a soil? Go ask thine aching heart, when sorrow from a thousand causes wounds it, go ask thy sickened self, when every medicine fails, whether this be the case or not?

Letter to the Abbé Raynal, 1782

Misfortune

❧

Misfortune and experience are lost upon mankind when they produce neither reflection nor reformation. Evils, like poisons, have their uses, and there are diseases which no other remedy can reach.

The Crisis, 1778

Misfortune and experience have now taught us system and method.

Common Sense on George III's Speech, 1782

Misfortune ever separates men in a bad cause, and unites them in a good one.

The Necessity of Taxation, 1782

Mistakes

As we have learned knowledge from misfortune, let us likewise learn it from mistake.

The Necessity of Taxation, 1782

Misuse of Words

It will always happen, that the nicest construction that words are capable of, when applied to the description of some thing which either cannot exist, or is too incomprehensible to be within the compass of description, will be words of sound only, and though they may amuse the ear, they cannot inform the mind.

Common Sense, 1776

Mixed Government

A mixed Government is an imperfect everything, cementing and soldering the discordant parts together by corruption, to act as a whole. . . . In mixed Governments there is no responsibility: the parts cover each other till responsibility is lost.

Rights of Man, I, 1791

Moderation

❦

There are men, in all countries, in whom both vice and virtue are kept subordinate by a kind of cowardice, which often forms a great part of that natural character styled *moderation*.

Pennsylvania Packet, January 28, 1779

A thing moderately good is not so good as it ought to be. Moderation in temper is always a virtue; but moderation in principle is always a vice.

Rights of Man, II, 1792

Monarchy

❦

Monarchical governments . . . are never long at rest; the crown itself is a temptation to enterprising ruffians at *home;* and that degree of pride and insolence ever attendant on regal authority, swells into a rupture with foreign powers, in instances, where a republican government, by being formed on more natural principles, would negotiate the mistake.

Common Sense, 1776

It is the pride of kings which throw mankind into confusion.

Common Sense, 1776

A thirst for absolute power is the natural disease of monarchy.

Common Sense, 1776

There is something exceedingly ridiculous in the composition of monarchy; it first excludes a man from the means of information, yet empowers him to act in cases where the highest judgment is required. The state of a king shuts him from the world, yet the business of a king requires him to know it thoroughly; wherefore the different parts, by unnaturally opposing and destroying each other, prove the whole character to be absurd and useless.

Common Sense, 1776

Government by kings . . . was the most prosperous invention the Devil ever set on foot for the promotion of idolatry. The Heathens paid divine honors to their deceased kings, and the christian world hath improved on the plan by doing the same to their living ones. How impious is the title of sacred majesty applied to a worm, who in the midst of his splendor is crumbling into dust!

Common Sense, 1776

Monarchy in every instance is the Popery of government.

Common Sense, 1776

Men who look upon themselves born to reign, and others to obey, soon grow insolent; selected from the rest of mankind their minds are early poisoned by importance; and the world they act in differs so materially from the world at large, that they have but little opportunity of knowing its true interests, and when they succeed to the government are frequently the most ignorant and unfit of any throughout the dominions.

Common Sense, 1776

Although they [i.e., kings] are beings of our *own* creating, they know not *us*, and are become the gods of their creators.

Common Sense, 1776

Nature seems sometimes to laugh at mankind, by giving them so many fools for Kings; at other times, she punishes their folly by giving them tyrants; but England must have offended highly to be cursed with both in one.

The Forester's Letters, 1776

Surely! there must be something strangely degenerating in the love of monarchy, that can so completely wear a man down to an ingrate, and make him proud to lick the dust that kings have trod upon.

The American Crisis, 1777

I have likewise an aversion to monarchy, as being too debasing to the dignity of man.

The American Crisis, 1777

I am not the personal enemy of Kings. Quite the contrary. No man more heartily wishes than myself to see them all in the happy and honorable state of private individuals; but I am the avowed, open, and intrepid enemy of what is called Monarchy; and I am such by principles which nothing can either alter or corrupt—by my attachment to humanity; by the anxiety which I feel within myself, for the dignity and the honor of the human race; by the disgust which I experience, when I observe men directed by children, and governed by brutes; by the horror which all the evils that Monarchy has spread over the earth excite within my breast; and by those sentiments which make me shudder at the calamities, the exactions, the wars, and the massacres with which Monarchy has crushed mankind: in short, it is against all the hell of monarchy that I have declared war.

To the Abbé Sieyes, Paris, July 8, 1791

Monarchy . . . is the popery of government; a thing kept up to amuse the ignorant, and quiet them into taxes.

Rights of Man, II, 1792

When it is laid down as a maxim, that *a King can do no wrong*, it places him in a state of similar security with that of idiots and persons insane, and responsibility is out of the question with respect to himself.

Rights of Man, II, 1792

What is the history of all monarchical governments, but a disgustful picture of human wretchedness, and the accidental respite of a few years repose?

Rights of Man, II, 1792

What is called the splendor of a throne is no other than the corruption of the state. It is made up of a band of parasites, living in luxurious indolence, out of the public taxes.

Rights of Man, II, 1792

Monarchy would not have continued so many ages in the world, had it not been for the abuses it protects. It is the master fraud, which shelters all others.

Rights of Man, II, 1792

All the monarchical governments are military. War is their trade, plunder and revenue their objects. While such government continue, peace has not the absolute security of a day.

Rights of Man, II, 1792

Kings are monsters in the natural order, and what can we expect from monsters but miseries and crimes?

An Essay for the Use of New Republicans, 1792

My hatred and abhorrence of monarchy are sufficiently known; they originate in principles of Reason and Conviction, nor, except with life, can they ever be extirpated.

Speech to the French National Convention, January 15, 1793

Monarchy, whatever form it may assume, arbitrary or otherwise, becomes necessarily a center, round which are united every species of corruption.

Speech to the French National Convention, January 15, 1793

Moral Goodness

That the moral duty of man consists in imitating the moral goodness and beneficence of God manifested in the creation towards all his creatures. That seeing, as we daily do, the goodness of God to all men, it is an example calling upon all men to practice the same towards each other; and consequently that every thing of persecution and revenge between man and man, and every thing of cruelty to animals, is a violation of moral duty.

Age of Reason, I, 1794

Morality

It is to my advantage that I have served an apprenticeship to life. I know the value of moral instruction, and I have seen the danger of the contrary.

Rights of Man, II, 1792

Morality is injured by prescribing to it duties, that, in the first place, are impossible to be performed, and if they could be, would be productive of evil; or . . . be premiums for crime.

Age of Reason, I, 1794

As for morality, the knowledge of it exists in every man's conscience.

Age of Reason, II, 1795

Motivation

As a bad cause cannot be prosecuted with a good motive, so neither can a good cause be long supported by a bad one.

Letter to the Abbé Raynal, 1782

A little matter will move a party, but it must be something great that moves a nation.

Rights of Man, II, 1792

Movement of the Human Body

❧ ❧

Man governs the whole when he pleases to govern, but in the interim the several parts, like little suburbs, govern themselves without consulting the sovereign.

An Essay on Dreams, 1802

National Character

❧ ❧

A good opinion of ourselves is exceedingly necessary in public life, and of the utmost importance in supporting national character.

The American Crisis, 1778

There is nothing sets the character of a nation in a higher or lower light with others, than the faithfully fulfilling, or perfidiously breaking of treaties. They are things not to be tampered with.

The Crisis, 1782

Let a nation conceive rightly of its character, and it will be chastely just in protecting it.

The Crisis, 1783

National Honor

❧ ❧

There is such an idea existing in the world as that of *national honor,* and this, falsely understood, is oftentimes the cause of war.

The Crisis, 1778

As individuals we profess ourselves christians, but as nations we are heathens.

The Crisis, 1778

National Reputation

❧ ❦

A fair national reputation is of as much importance as independence. That it possesses a charm which wins upon the world, and makes even enemies civil. That it gives a dignity which is often superior to power, and commands a reverence where pomp and splendor fail.

The Crisis, 1783

National Sins

❧ ❦

There are such things as national sins, and though the punishment of individuals may be reserved to *another* world, national punishment can only be inflicted in *this* world.

The American Crisis, 1777

All countries have sooner or later been called to their reckoning; the proudest empires have sunk when the balance was struck.

The American Crisis, 1777

Nationalism

❧ ❦

Always remembering, that our strength is continental, not provincial.

Common Sense, 1776

Nations

A nation, though continually existing, is continually in a state of renewal and succession. It is never stationary. Every day produces new births, carries minors forward to maturity, and old persons from the stage.

Dissertation on First Principles of Government, 1795

Natural Rights

A *natural* right is an animal right; and the power to act it, is supposed, either fully or in part, to be mechanically contained within ourselves as individuals. *Civil* rights are derived from the assistance or agency of other persons; they form a sort of common stock, which, by raw consent of all, may be occasionally used for the benefit of any.

Candid and Critical Remarks on a Letter Signed Ludlow, 1777

The error of those who reason by precedents drawn from antiquity, respecting the *rights of man*, is, that they do not go far enough into antiquity. They do not go the whole way. They stop in some of the intermediate stages of an hundred or a thousand years, and produce what was then done as a rule for the present day. This is no authority at all. If we travel still farther into antiquity, we shall find a direct contrary opinion and practice prevailing; and if antiquity is to be authority, a thousand such authorities may be produced, successively contradicting each other: But if we proceed on, we shall at last come out right; we shall come to the time when man came from the hand of his Maker. What was he then? Man. Man was his high and only title, and a higher cannot be given him.

Rights of Man, I, 1791

The genealogy of Christ is traced to Adam. Why then not trace the *rights of man* to the creation of man? I will answer the question. Because there have been an upstart of governments, thrusting themselves between, and presumptuously working to *unmake* man.

Rights of Man, I, 1791

Every history of the creation, and every traditionary account, whether from the lettered or unlettered world, however they may vary in their opinion or belief of certain particulars, all agree in establishing one point, *the unity of man;* by which I mean that man is all of *one degree*, and consequently that all men are born equal, and with equal natural rights, in the same manner as if posterity had been continued by *creation* instead of *generation*, the latter being only the mode by which the former is carried forward; and consequently, every child born into the world must be considered as deriving its existence from God. The world is as new to him as it was to the first man that existed, and his natural right in it is of the same kind.

Rights of Man, I, 1791

Natural rights are those which appertain to man in right of his existence. Of this kind are all the intellectual rights, or rights of the mind, and also all those rights of acting as an individual for his own comfort and happiness, which are not injurious to the natural rights of others.—Civil rights are those which appertain to man in right of his being a member of society. Every civil right has for its foundation some natural right pre-existing in the individual, but to which his individual power is not, in all cases, sufficiently competent. Of this kind are all those which relate to security and protection.

Rights of Man, I, 1791

The natural rights which he [i.e., man] retains, are all those in which the *power* to execute is as perfect in the individual as the right itself. Among this class, as is before mentioned, are all the intellectual rights, or rights of the mind; consequently, religion is one of those rights. The natural rights which are not retained, are all those in which, though the right is perfect in the individual, the power to execute them is defective. They answer not his purpose. A man, by natural right, has a right to judge in his own cause; and so far as the right of the mind is concerned, he never surrenders it: But what availeth it him to judge, if he has not power to redress? He therefore deposits this right in the common stock of society, and takes the arm of society, of which he is a part, in preference and in addition to his own. Society *grants* him nothing. Every man is a proprietor in society, and draws on the capital as a matter of right.

Rights of Man, I, 1791

Nature

%ᒷ Ӌ%

He who takes nature for his guide is not easily beaten out of his argument.

Common Sense, 1776

There are but two natural sources of wealth and strength—the earth and the ocean.

Peace, and the Newfoundland Fisheries, 1779

Nature is orderly in all her works.

Rights of Man, II, 1792

But if objects for gratitude and admiration are our desire, do they not present themselves every hour to our eyes? Do we not see a fair creation prepared to receive us the instant we were born—a world furnished to our hands that cost us nothing? Is it we that light up the sun; that pour down the rain; and fill the earth with abundance? Whether we sleep or wake, the vast machinery of the universe still goes on.

Age of Reason, I, 1794

Every thing we behold is, in one sense, a mystery to us. Our own existence is a mystery: the whole vegetable world is a mystery. We cannot account how it is that an acorn, when put into the ground, is made to develop itself, and become an oak. We know not how it is that the seed we sow unfolds and multiplies itself, and returns to us such an abundant interest for so small a capital.

Age of Reason, I, 1794

Navies

❧ ❦

No country on the globe is so happily situated, or so internally capable of raising a fleet as America.

Common Sense, 1776

We ought to view the building a fleet as an article of commerce, it being the natural manufactory of this country. It is the best money we can lay out. A navy when finished is worth more than it cost. And is that nice point in national policy, in which commerce and protection are united.

Common Sense, 1776

To unite the sinews of commerce and defense is sound policy; for when our strength and our riches, play into each other's hand, we need fear no external enemy.

Common Sense, 1776

With respect to Navies, they are of a Nature different in their operation to Armies. They are limited to the Sea. They cannot be employed to the purposes of internal despotism. They can neither make nor overturn revolutions. They are Fishes, and though a whale might swallow a Jonah at Sea it could not hurt a pismire at land.

To William Short, June 1, 1790

Naysayers

❧ ❦

I hate a prophesier of ill-luck, because the pride of being thought wise often carries him to the wrong side.

Peace, and the Newfoundland Fisheries, 1779

Necessity

Immediate necessity makes many things convenient, which if continued would grow into oppression.

Common Sense, 1776

Neutrality

Neutrality . . . would be a safer convoy than a man of war.

Common Sense, 1776

New Discoveries

It is with Gravitation, as it is with all new discoveries, it is applied to explain too many things.

To Thomas Jefferson, May 1788

New Thinking

Put man in a situation that requires new thinking, and the mind will grow up to it, for, like the body, it improves by exercise. Man is but a learner all his lifetime.

To the People of England on the Invasion of England, 1798

Newspapers

The manners of a nation, or of a party, can be better ascertained from the character of its press than from any other public circumstance. If its press is licentious, its manners are not good. Nobody believes a common liar, or a common defamer.

Liberty of the Press, 1806

Nonsense

Nonsense ought to be treated as nonsense wherever it be found.

Predestination, 1809

Oaths

If a government requires the support of oaths, it is a sign that it is not worth supporting, and ought not to be supported. Make government what it ought to be, and it will support itself.

Rights of Man, II, 1792

Obligation

To oblige and be obliged is fair work among mankind, and we want an opportunity of showing to the world that we are a people sensible of kindness and worthy of confidence.

The Crisis, 1782

Obstinacy

❧ ❧

There is something in obstinacy which differs from every other passion, whenever it fails it never recovers, but either breaks like iron or crumbles sulkily away like a fractured arch. Most other passions have their periods of fatigue and rest; their suffering and their cure; but obstinacy has no resource, and the first wound is mortal.

The Crisis, 1778

Old Age

❧ ❧

They have arrived at their second childhood, the infancy of three score and ten.

The Forester's Letters, 1776

To be happy in old age, it is necessary that we accustom ourselves to objects that can accompany the mind all the way through life, and that we take the rest as good in their day. The man of pleasure is miserable in old age, and the mere drudge in business is but little better: whereas natural philosophy, mathematical, and mechanical science, are a continual source of tranquil pleasure . . . Those who knew Benjamin Franklin will recollect that his mind was ever young; his temper ever serene. Science, that never grows grey, was always his mistress. He was never without an object; for when we cease to have an object, we become like an invalid in an hospital waiting for death.

Age of Reason, II, 1795

Openness

✿

A government or an administration, who means and acts honestly, has nothing to fear, and consequently has nothing to conceal.

Common Sense on Financing the War, 1782

The opener and fairer public business is transacted, the better it succeeds. Where no fraud is intended, there can be no occasion for concealment, and it is not only necessary that measures should be just, but that everybody should know them to be so.

The Necessity of Taxation, 1782

I never do anything that I wish to conceal.

Philadelphia *Freeman's Journal*, May 1, 1782

Opinion

✿

Error in opinion has this peculiar advantage with it, that the foremost point of the contrary ground may at any time be reached by the sudden exertion of a thought; and it frequently happens in sentimental differences that some striking circumstance, or some forcible reason, quickly conceived, will effect in an instant what neither argument nor example could produce in an age.

The American Crisis, 1777

It might be said, that until men think for themselves the whole is prejudice, and *not opinion*; for that only is opinion which is the result of reason and reflection.

Rights of Man, II, 1792

I have always strenuously supported the Right of every Man to his own opinion, however different that opinion might be to mine. He who denies to another this right, makes a slave of himself to his present opinion, because he precludes himself the right of changing it.

Age of Reason, I, 1794

Every man has a *right to give an opinion*, but no man has a right that his own should govern the rest.

Dissertation on First Principles of Government, 1795

Opportunism

Men cannot, properly speaking, make circumstances for his purpose, but he always has it in his power to improve them when they occur.

Rights of Man, I, 1791

Oppression

Oppression is often the *consequence*, but seldom or never the *means* of riches.

Common Sense, 1776

When men are sore with the sense of oppressions, and menaced with the prospect of new ones, is the calmness of philosophy, or the palsy of insensibility, to be looked for?

Rights of Man, I, 1791

Order

❦

Governments, so far from being always the cause or means of order, are often the destruction of it.

Rights of Man, II, 1792

Origins

❦

It is by tracing things to their origins that we learn to understand them: and it is by keeping that line and that origin always in view that we never forget them.

Dissertation on First Principles of Government, 1795

It is only by tracing things to their origin, that we can gain rightful ideas of them, and it is by gaining such ideas that we discover the boundary that divides right from wrong, and which teaches every man to know his own.

Agrarian Justice, 1797

Panics

❦

'Tis surprising to see how rapidly a panic will sometimes run through a country. All nations and ages have been subject to them: . . . Yet panics, in some cases, have their uses; they produce as much good as hurt. Their duration is always short; the mind soon grows through them, and acquires a firmer habit than before. But their peculiar advantage is, that they are the touchstones of sincerity and hypocrisy, and bring things and men to light, which might otherwise have lain for ever undiscovered.

The American Crisis, 1776

Parenting

❧

Nothing hurts the affections both of parents and children so much, as living too closely connected, and keeping up the distinction too long. Domineering will not do over those, who by a progress in life are become equal in rank to their parents, that is, when they have families of their own; and though they may conceive themselves the subjects of their advice, will not suppose themselves the objects of their government.

The Crisis, 1778

Passion

❧

When the governing passion of any man or set of men is once known, the method of managing them is easy; for even misers, whom no public virtue can impress, would become generous, could a heavy tax be laid upon covetousness.

The American Crisis, 1777

Every passion that acts upon mankind has a peculiar mode of operation. Many of them are temporary and fluctuating; they admit of cessation and variety.

The Crisis Extraordinary, 1780

Past Hardships

❧

What are the little sufferings of the present day, compared with the hardships that are past.

Common Sense on George III's Speech, 1782

Patriotism

❧ ❧

There is not a vice, and scarcely a virtue, that has not as the fashion of the moment suited been called by the name of patriotism. . . . But if we give to patriotism a fixed idea consistent with that of a republic, it would signify a strict adherence to the principles of moral justice, to the equality of civil and political rights, to the system of representative government, and an opposition to every hereditary claim to govern; and of this species of patriotism you know my character.

To James Monroe, October 20, 1794

Peace

❧ ❧

A government which cannot preserve the peace, is no government at all.

Common Sense, 1776

The love and desire of peace is not confined to Quakerism, it is the *natural*, as well as the religious wish of all denominations of men.

Common Sense, 1776

Our plan is peace forever.

Common Sense, 1776

If peace can be procured with more advantages than even a conquest can be obtained, he must be an idiot indeed that hesitates.

The Crisis, 1778

Peace is easy if willingly set about.

The Crisis, 1778

Peace, to every reflecting mind, is a desirable object; but *that peace* which is accompanied with a ruined character, becomes a crime to the seducer, and a curse upon the seduced.

Letter to the Abbé Raynal, 1782

The rage for conquest has had its fashion, and its day. Why may not the amiable virtues have the same? The Alexander and Caesars of antiquity have left behind them their monuments of destruction, and are remembered with hatred; while those more exalted characters, who first taught society and science, are blessed with the gratitude of every age and country. Of more use was *one* philosopher, though a heathen, to the world, than all the heathen conquerors that ever existed.

Letter to the Abbé Raynal, 1782

Peace, which costs nothing, is attended with infinitely more advantage, than any victory with all its expence.

Rights of Man, II, 1792

The People

The mind of a *living* public is quickly alarmed and easily tormented.

The Affair of Silas Deane, 1778

Petitioning

Nothing flatters vanity, or confirms obstinacy in Kings more than repeated petitioning.

Common Sense, 1776

Philanthropy

❦

The more we bestow the richer we become.

The Crisis Extraordinary, 1780

Political Failure

❦

A long series of politics so remarkably distinguished by a succession of misfortunes, without one alleviating turn, must certainly have something in it systematically wrong. It is sufficient to awaken the most credulous into suspicion, and the most obstinate into thought.

The Crisis, 1778

Political Parties

❦

The little wranglings and indecent contentions of personal party, are as dishonorable to our characters, as they are injurious to our repose.

The Crisis, 1783

Party knows no impulse but spirit, no prize but victory. It is blind to truth, and hardened against conviction. It seeks to justify error by perseverance, and denies to its own mind the operation of its own judgment. A man under the tyranny of party spirit is the greatest slave upon earth, for none but himself can deprive him of the freedom of thought.

To the Opposers of the Bank, 1787

It is the nature and intention of a constitution to *prevent governing by party*, by establishing a common principle that shall limit and control the power and impulse of party, and that says to all parties, *thus far shalt thou go and no further*. But in the absence of a constitution, men look entirely to party; and instead of principle governing party, party governs principle.

Dissertation on First Principles of Government, 1795

In the history of parties and the names they assume, it often happens, that they finish by the direct contrary principles with which they profess to begin.

To the Citizens of the United States, 1802

Politics

❦

A narrow system of politics, like a narrow system of religion, is calculated only to sour the temper, and live at variance with mankind.

The American Crisis, 1777

Politics to be executively right, must have a unity of means and time, and a defect in either overthrows the whole.

The Crisis, 1778

Whenever politics are applied to debauch mankind from their integrity, and dissolve the virtue of human nature, they become detestable; and to be a statesman on this plan, is to be a commissioned villain. He who aims at it, leaves a vacancy in his character, which may be filled up with the worst of epithets.

Letter to the Abbé Raynal, 1782

Popularity

That which is right will become popular, and that which is wrong, though by mistake it may obtain the cry or fashion of the day, will soon lose the power of delusion, and sink into disesteem.

Common Sense on Financing the War, 1782

I have never yet made, and I hope I never shall make, it the least point of consideration, whether a thing is *popular* or *unpopular*, but whether it is *right* or *wrong*. That which is right will become popular, and that which is wrong will soon lose its temporary popularity, and sink into disgrace.

A Friend to Rhode-Island and the Union, 1783

As he rose like a rocket, he would fall like the stick.

Common Sense on Financing the War, 1782;
A Friend to Rhode-Island and the Union, 1783

There are two distinct species of popularity: the one excited by merit, the other by resentment.

Rights of Man, I, 1791

Positive Construction

It is incumbent upon us, and contributes also to our own tranquility, that we put the best construction upon a thing it will bear.

Age of Reason, II, 1795

Posterity

❧ ❧

When we are planning for posterity, we ought to remember, that virtue is not hereditary.

Common Sense, 1776

If there must be trouble let it be in my day, that my child may have peace.

The American Crisis, 1776

Potential

❧ ❧

There is existing in man, a mass of sense lying in a dormant state, and which, unless something excites it to action, will descend with him, in that condition, to the grave.

Rights of Man, II, 1792

Poverty

❧ ❧

Poverty . . . is a thing created by that which is called civilized life. It exists not in the natural state.

Agrarian Justice, 1797

It is the practice of what has unjustly obtained the name of civilization (and the practice merits not to be called either charity or policy) to make some provision for persons becoming poor and wretched, only at the time they become so. Would it not, even as a matter of economy, be far better, to devise means to prevent their becoming poor.

Agrarian Justice, 1797

The great mass of the poor, in all countries, are become an hereditary race, and it is next to impossible for them to get out of that state
of themselves. It ought also to be observed, that this mass increases
in all the countries that are called civilized. More persons fall annually into it, than get out of it.

Agrarian Justice, 1797

Power

❧

A long and violent abuse of power, is generally the Means of calling
the right of it in question.

Common Sense, 1776

We repose an unwise confidence in any government, or in any men,
when we invest them officially with too much, or an unnecessary
quantity of, discretionary power; for though we might clearly con-
fide in almost any man of the present age, yet we ought ever to remember that virtue is not hereditary either in the office or in the
persons.

A Serious Address to the People of Pennsylvania, 1778

Uncontrolled power, in the hands of an incensed, imperious and ra-
pacious conqueror, is an engine of dreadful execution; and woe be to
that country over which it can be exercised.

The Crisis Extraordinary, 1780

The abuse of any power always operates to call the right of that
power in question.

Attack on Paper Money Laws, 1786

The substantial basis of the power of a nation arises out of its population, its wealth and its revenues. To these may be added the disposition of the people.

Prospects on the Rubicon, 1787

Immortal power is not a human right.

Rights of Man, I, 1791

All power exercised over a nation, must have some beginning. It must be either delegated, or assumed. There are no other sources. All delegated power is trust, and all assumed power is usurpation. Time does not alter the nature and quality of either.

Rights of Man, II, 1792

Those who abuse liberty when they possess it would abuse power could they obtain it.

To the Citizens of the United States, 1802

Prayer

A man does not serve God when he prays, for it is himself he is trying to serve . . . but instead of buffeting the Deity with prayers as if I distrusted him or must dictate to him, I reposed myself on his protection; and you, my friend, will find, even in your last moments, more consolation in the silence of resignation than in the murmuring wish of prayer.

To Samuel Adams, Washington, January 1, 1803

Precedents

We are now got at the origin of man, and at the origin of his rights. As to the manner in which the world has been governed from that day to this, is no farther any concern of ours than to make a proper use of the errors or the improvements which the history of it presents. Those who lived a hundred or a thousand years ago, were then moderns as we are now. They had *their* ancients, and those ancients had others, and we also shall be ancients in our turn. If the mere name of antiquity is to govern in the affairs of life, the people who are to live an hundred or a thousand years hence, may as well take us for a precedent, as we make a precedent of those who lived an hundred or a thousand years ago. The fact is, that portions of antiquity, by proving every thing, establish nothing. It is authority against authority all the way, till we come to the divine origins of the *rights of man* at the creation. Here our enquiries find a resting-place, and our reason finds a home. If a dispute about the *rights of man* had arose at the distance of an hundred years from the creation, it is to this source of authority they must have referred, and it is to the same source of authority that we must now refer.

Rights of Man, I, 1791

Governments by precedent, without any regard to the principle of the precedent, is one of the vilest systems that can be set up.

Rights of Man, II, 1792

Either the doctrine of precedents is policy to keep man in a state of ignorance, or it is a practical concession that wisdom degenerates in governments as governments increase in age, and can only hobble along by the stilts and crutches of precedents. How is it that the same persons who would proudly be thought wiser than their predecessors, appear at the same time only as the ghosts of departed wisdom? How strangely is antiquity treated? To answer some purposes it is spoken of as the times of darkness and ignorance, and to answer others, it is put for the light of the world.

Rights of Man, II, 1792

Predestination

The absurd and impious doctrine of *predestination*, a doctrine destructive of morals, would never have been thought of had it not been for some stupid passages in the Bible, which priestcraft at first, and ignorance since, have imposed upon mankind as revelation.

Predestination, 1809

Predictions

❦

I am not fond of hazarding opinions, neither is it proper or prudent to do it.

To Thomas Jefferson, September 9, 1788

Prejudice

❦

It is difficult to get over local or long standing prejudices.

Common Sense, 1776

We are never in a proper condition of doing justice to others, while we continue under the influence of some leading partiality, so neither are we capable of doing it to ourselves while we remain fettered by any obstinate prejudice.

Common Sense, 1776

It frequently happens that in proportion as we are taught to dislike persons and countries not knowing why, we feel an ardor of esteem upon a removal of the mistake. It seems as if something was to be made amends for, and we eagerly give into every office of friendship to atone for the injury of the error.

The Crisis, 1780

There is something exceedingly curious in the constitution and operation of prejudice. It has the singular ability of accommodating itself to all the possible varieties of the human mind. Some passions and vices are but thinly scattered among mankind, and find only here and there a fitness of reception. But prejudice, like the spider, makes every place its home. It has neither taste nor choice of situation, and all that it requires is room. Everywhere, except in fire or water, a spider will live.

So, let the mind be as naked as the walls of an empty and forsaken tenement, gloomy as a dungeon, or ornamented with the richest abilities of thinking, let it be hot, cold, dark or light, lonely or inhabited, still prejudice, if undisturbed, will fill it with cobwebs, and live, like the spider, where there seems nothing to live on. If the one prepares her food by poisoning it to her palate and her use, the other does the same; and as several of our passions are strongly characterized by the animal world, prejudice may be denominated the spider of the mind.

Letter to the Abbé Raynal, 1782

No man is prejudiced in favor of a thing, knowing it to be wrong. He is attached to it on the belief of its being right; and when he sees it is not so, the prejudice will be gone. We have but a defective idea of what prejudice is. It might be said, that until men think for themselves the whole is prejudice, and *not opinion*; for that only is opinion which is the result of reason and reflection.

Rights of Man, II, 1792

Prejudice will fall in a combat with interest.

Rights of Man, II, 1792

Preparation

✳ ✳

The best of arguments is a vigorous preparation.

Address to the People of France, 1792

The Press

✳ ✳

There is nothing which obtains so general an influence over the manners and morals of a people as the press; from *that* as from a fountain, the streams of vice or virtue are poured forth over a country.

The Pennsylvania Magazine, I, 1775

Pride

❧

Our pride is always hurt by the same propositions which offend our principles: for when we are shocked at the crime we are wounded by the supposition of our compliance.

The Crisis, 1782

Principle

❧

To be *nobly wrong* is more manly than to be *meanly right*. Only let the error be disinterested—let it wear, *not the mask*, but the *mark* of principle and 'tis pardonable.

The Forester's Letters, 1776

My principles are universal. My attachment is to all the world and not to any particular part, and if what I advance is right, no matter where or who it comes from.

The Crisis, 1778

Principles deserve to be remembered, and to remember them rightly is repossessing them.

The Crisis Extraordinary, 1780

To be *nobly wrong is more manly than to be meanly right,* is an expression I once used on a former occasion, and it is equally applicable now. We feel something like respect for consistency even in error. We lament the virtue that is debauched into a vice, but the vice that affects a virtue becomes the more detestable: and amongst the various assumptions of character, which hypocrisy has taught, and men have practiced, there is none that raises a higher relish of disgust, than to see disappointed inveteracy twisting itself, by the most visible falsehoods, into an appearance of piety it has no pretensions to.

Common Sense on George III's Speech, 1782

Principle, like truth, needs no contrivance.

Letter to the Abbé Raynal, 1782

Men who act from principle, however separated by circumstances, will, without contrivance, act alike, and the concurrence of their conduct is an evidence of their rectitude.

To Elias Boudinot, June 7, 1783

The true greatness of a nation is founded on the principles of humanity.

Prospects on the Rubicon, 1787

When a man in a long cause attempts to steer his course by any thing else than some polar truth or principle, he is sure to be lost. It is beyond the compass of his capacity, to keep all the parts of an argument together, and make them unite in one issue, by any other means than having this guide always in view. Neither memory nor invention will supply the want of it. The former fails him, and the latter betrays him.

Rights of Man, I, 1791

I think it equally as injurious to good principles to permit them to linger, as to push them on too fast.

Rights of Man, II, 1792

When principle, and not place, is the energetic cause of action, a man, I find, is every where the same.

Rights of Man, II, 1792

Principles must stand on their own merits, and if they are good they certainly will.

Rights of Man, II, 1792

The interference of foreign despots may serve to introduce into their own enslaved countries the principles that they come to oppose.

Letter to the People of France, 1792

It is not because right principles have been violated that they are to be abandoned.

Age of Reason, II, 1795

Man cannot make principles; he can only discover them.

Age of Reason, I, 1794

Principles which are influenced and subject to the control of tyranny have not their foundation in the heart.

Speech to the French National Convention, July 7, 1795

When men depart from an established principle, they are compelled to resort to trick and subterfuge, always shifting their means to preserve the unity of their objects; and as it rarely happens that the first expedient makes amends for the prostitution of principle, they must call in aid a second of a more flagrant nature to supply the deficiency of the former. In this manner legislators go on accumulating error upon error, and artifice upon artifice, until the mass becomes so bulky and incongruous, and their embarrassment so desperate, that they are compelled, as their last expedient, to resort to the very principle they had violated.

Speech to the French National Convention, 1795

An army of principles will penetrate where an army of soldiers cannot—It will succeed where diplomatic management would fail—It is neither Rhine, the Channel, nor the Ocean, that can arrest its progress—It will march on the horizon of the world, and it will conquer.

Agrarian Justice, 1797

Man cannot make, or invent, or contrive principles; he can only discover them, and he ought to look through the discovery to the Author.

A Discourse at the Society of Theophilanthropists, 1797

Printing

The art of printing changes all the cases, and opens a scene as vast as the world. It gives to man a sort of divine attribute. It gives to him mental omnipresence. He can be everywhere and at the same instant; for wherever he is read he is mentally there.

A Reply to the Bishop of Llandaff, 1802

Private Property

That property will ever be unequal is certain. Industry, superiority of talents, dexterity of management, extreme frugality, fortunate opportunities, or the opposite, or the means of those things, will ever produce that effect, without having recourse to the harsh, ill-sounding names of avarice and oppression.

Dissertation on First Principles of Government, 1795

When rights are secure, property is secure in consequence.

Dissertation on First Principles of Government, 1795

There could be no such thing as landed property originally. Man did not make the earth, and, though he had a natural right to *occupy* it, he had no right to *locate* as *his property* in perpetuity on any part of it.

Agrarian Justice, 1797

Procrastination

The longer it is delayed the harder it will be to accomplish.

Common Sense, 1776

Progress

Man advances from idea to idea, from thought to thought, and all the time he is unaware of his marvelous progress.

Answers to Four Questions on Legislative and Executive Powers, 1791

Protection for Citizens Abroad

It is the duty of every government to charge itself with the care of any of its citizens who may happen to fall under an arbitrary persecution abroad.

To George Washington, August 3, 1796

Prudence

Right by chance and wrong by system are things so frequently seen in the political world, that it becomes a proof of prudence neither to censure nor applaud too soon.

Prospects on the Rubicon, 1787

Prudence is, in many cases, a substitute for principle, and is so nearly allied to hypocrisy, that it easily sides into it.

To George Washington, August 3, 1796

Public Character

❦

The man who is a *good* public character from *craft*, and not from moral principle, if such a character can be called *good*, is not much to be depended on.

To John Fellows, July 31, 1805

Public Debt

❦

No nation ought to be without a debt. A national debt is a national bond.

Common Sense, 1776

Public Opinion

❦

I shall so far take the sense of the public for my guide.

Rights of Man, II, 1792

Public Policy

❦

The success of any proposed plan, submitted to public consideration, must finally depend on the numbers interested in supporting it, united with the justice of its principles.

Agrarian Justice, 1797

Public Service

❧ ❦

Every man who acts beyond the line of private life, must expect to pass through two severe examinations. First, as to his motives; secondly, as to his conduct: On the former of these depends his character for honesty; on the latter for wisdom.

Four Letters on Interesting Subjects, 1776

I am sensible that he who means to do mankind a real service must set down with the determination of putting up, and bearing with all their faults, follies, prejudices and mistakes until he can convince them that he is right, and that his object is a general good.

To Robert Morris, February 20, 1782

Public Spirit

❧ ❦

Where men have not public spirit to render themselves serviceable, it ought to be the study of government to draw the best use possible from their vices. When the governing passion of any man or set of men is once known, the method of managing them is easy; for even misers, whom no public virtue can impress, would become generous, could a heavy tax be laid upon covetousness.

The American Crisis, 1777

There are many men who will do their duty when it is not wanted; but a genuine Public spirit always appears most when there is most occasion for it.

The American Crisis, 1777

Punishments

An avidity to punish is always dangerous to liberty. It leads men to stretch, to misinterpret and to misapply even the best of laws.

Dissertation on First Principles of Government, 1795

Quakers

The principles of Quakerism have a direct tendency to make a man the quiet and inoffensive subject of any, and every government *which is set over him*.

Common Sense, 1776

What more can we say of ye than that a religious Quaker is a valuable character, and a political Quaker a real Jesuit.

The American Crisis, 1777

The religion that approaches the nearest of all others to true deism, in the moral and benign part thereof, is that professed by the quakers, but they have contracted themselves too much by leaving the works of God out of their system. Though I reverence their philanthropy, I cannot help smiling at the conceit, that if the taste of a quaker could have been consulted at the creation, what a silent and drab-colored creation it would have been! Not a flower would have blossomed its gaieties, nor a bird been permitted to sing.

Age of Reason, I, 1794

The only sect that has not persecuted, are the Quakers, and the only reason that can be given for it is, that they are rather Deists than Christians. They do not believe much about Jesus Christ, and they call the scriptures a dead letter.

Age of Reason, II, 1795

Qualifications for Officeholding

❦

Common sense, common honesty and civil manners qualify a man for government and, besides this, put man in a situation that requires new thinking, and the mind will grow up to it, for, like the body, it improves by exercise. Man is but a learner all his lifetime.

To the People of England on the Invasion of England, 1798

Quotations

❦

I scarcely ever quote; the reason is, I always think.

The Forester's Letters, 1776

Rage

❦

Nothing is more ridiculous than ridiculous rage.

To the Citizens of the United States, 1802

Rashness

❦

When men have rashly plunged themselves into a measure, the right or wrong of it is soon forgotten.

To the Opposers of the Bank, 1787

Reason

❧ ❧

Reason and Ignorance, the opposites of each other, influence the great bulk of mankind. If either of these can be rendered sufficiently extensive in a country, the machinery of Government goes easily on. Reason obeys itself; and Ignorance submits to whatever is dictated to it.

Rights of Man, I, 1791

We will exercise the reason with which we are endued, or we possess it unworthily. As reason is given at all times, it is for the purpose of being used at all times.

Address and Declaration, 1791

Reason, like time, will make its own way, and prejudice will fall in a combat with interest.

Rights of Man, II, 1792

It would not only be wrong, but bad policy, to attempt by force what ought to be accomplished by reason.

Rights of Man, II, 1792

Reason and discussion will soon bring things right, however wrong they may begin.

Rights of Man, II, 1792

It may be considered as an honor to the animal faculties of man to obtain redress by courage and danger, but it is far greater honor to the rational faculties to accomplish the same object by reason, accommodation, and general consent.

Rights of Man, II, 1792

Fact is superior to reasoning.

Rights of Man, II, 1792

The most formidable weapon against errors of every kind is Reason. I have never used any other, and I trust I never shall.

Age of Reason, I, 1794

It is only by the exercise of reason, that man can discover God.

Age of Reason, I, 1794

Reasonableness

❦

As politicians we ought not so much to ground our hope on the reasonableness of the thing we ask, as on the reasonableness of the person of whom we ask it: Who would expect discretion from a fool, candor from a tyrant, or justice from a villain?

The American Crisis, 1777

Rebellion

❦

He that rebels against reason is a real rebel, but he that in defence of reason, rebels against tyranny, has a better title to "Defender of the Faith" than George the Third.

The American Crisis, 1777

Examples are not wanting to show how dreadfully vindictive and cruel are all old government, when they are successful against what they call a revolt.

Rights of Man, I, 1791

When all other rights are taken away the right of rebellion is made perfect.

Dissertation on First Principles of Government, 1795

Reform

❧

Nothing in the political world ought to be held improbable.
Rights of Man, I, 1791

Where we would wish to reform we must not reproach.
Rights of Man, II, 1792

Only partial advantages can flow from partial reforms.
Rights of Man, II, 1792

As to reformation, whenever it comes, it must be from the nation, and not from the government.
Rights of Man, II, 1792

Some reform must, from the necessity of the case, soon begin. It is not whether these principles press with little or much force in the present moment. They are out. They are abroad in the world, and no force can stop them. Like a secret told, they are beyond recall.
Rights of Man, II, 1792

Rejection

❧

To suppose a rejection is to invite it.
Peace, and the Newfoundland Fisheries, 1779

Religion

To God, and not to man, are all men accountable on the score of religion.

Common Sense, 1776; *Epistle to Quakers*, 1776

Every religion is good, that teaches man to be good.

Rights of Man, II, 1792

Religion is very improperly made a political machine.

Rights of Man, II, 1792

Religious duties consist in doing justice, loving mercy, and endeavoring to make our fellow creatures happy.

Age of Reason, I, 1794

Man does not learn religion as he learns the secrets and mysteries of a trade. He learns the theory of religion by reflection. It arises out of the action of his own mind upon the things which he sees, or upon what he may happen to hear or to read, and the practice joins itself thereto.

Age of Reason, I, 1794

The only true religion is deism, by which I . . . mean the belief of one God, and an imitation of his moral character, or the practice of what are called moral virtues.

Age of Reason, I, 1794

The creation is the bible of the deist. He there reads, in the hand writing of the Creator himself, the certainty of his existence, and the immutability of his power; and all other bibles and testaments are to him forgeries.

Age of Reason, II, 1795

Religion has two principal enemies, fanaticism and infidelity, or that which is called atheism. The first requires to be combated by reason and morality, the other by natural philosophy.

A Discourse at the Society of Theophilanthropists, 1797

The universe is the bible of a true Theophilanthropist. It is there that he reads God. It is there that the proofs of His existence are to be sought and to be found. . . . the universe [is] the true Bible—the inimitable work of God.

A Discourse at the Society of Theophilanthropists, 1797

The modes of worship are as various as the sects are numerous; and amidst all this variety and multiplicity there is but one article of belief in which every religion in the world agrees. That article has universal sanction. It is the belief of a God, or what the Greeks described by the word *Theism*, and the Latins by that of *Deism*.

A Letter to Camille Jordan, 1797

The intellectual part of religion is a private affair between every man and his Maker, and in which no third party has any right to interfere. The practical part consists in our doing good to each other.

A Letter to Camille Jordan, 1797

Religion does not unite itself to show and noise. True religion is without either. Where there is both there is no true religion.

A Letter to Camille Jordan, 1797

Practical religion consists in doing good; and the only way of serving God is, that of endeavoring to make his creation happy. All preaching that has not this for its object is nonsense and hypocrisy.

Agrarian Justice, 1797

The key to heaven is not in the keeping of any sect, nor ought the road to it to be obstructed by any. Our relation to each other in this world is as men, and the man who is a friend to man and to his rights, let his religious opinions be what they may, is a good citizen.

To Samuel Adams, Washington, January 1, 1803

Religious Diversity

It is the will of the Almighty, that there should be diversity of religious opinions among us: It affords a larger field for our Christian kindness. Were we all of one way of thinking, our religious dispositions would want matter for probation; and on this liberal principle, I look on the various denominations among us, to be like children of the same family, differing only, in what is called, their Christian names.

Common Sense, 1776

If we suppose a large family of children, who, on any particular day, or particular circumstance, made it a custom to present to their parent some token of their affection and gratitude, each of them would make a different offering, and most probably in a different manner. Some would pay their congratulations in themes of verse or prose, by some little devices, as their genius dictated, or according to what they thought would please; and, perhaps, the least of all, not able to do any of those things, would ramble into the garden, or the field, and gather what it thought the prettiest flower it could find, though, perhaps, it might be but a simple weed. The parent would be more gratified by such variety, than if the whole of them had acted on a concerted plan, and each had made exactly the same offering. This would have the cold appearance of contrivance, or the harsh one of controul. But of all unwelcome things, nothing could more afflict the parent than to know, that the whole of them had afterwards gotten together by the ears, boys and girls, fighting, scratching, reviling, and abusing each other about which was the best or the worst present.

Why may we not suppose, that the great Father of all is pleased with variety of devotion; and that the greatest offense we can act, is that by which we seek to torment and render each other miserable.

Rights of Man, II, 1792

I do not believe that any two men, on what are called doctrinal points, think alike who think at all. It is only those who have not thought that appear to agree.

Rights of Man, II, 1792

Adam, if ever there were such a man, was created a Deist; but in the mean time let every man follow, as he has a right to do, the religion and the worship he prefers.

Age of Reason, I, 1794

Religious Establishment

❧ ❦

All religions are in their nature mild and benign, and united with principles of morality. They could not have made proselites at first, by professing any thing that was vicious, cruel, persecuting, or immoral. Like every thing else, they had their beginning; and they proceeded by persuasion, exhortation, and example. How then is it that they lose their native mildness, and become morose and intolerant?

It proceeds from the connection which Mr. Burke recommends. By engendering the church with the state, a sort of mule animal, capable only of destroying, and not of breeding up, is produced, called *The Church established by Law*. It is a stranger, even from its birth, to any parent mother on which it is begotten, and whom in time it kicks out and destroys.

Rights of Man, I, 1791

Persecution is not an original feature in *any* religion; but it is always the strongly-marked feature of all law-religions, or religions established by law. Take away the law-establishment, and every religion reassumes its original benignity.

Rights of Man, I, 1791

All national institutions of churches, whether Jewish, Christian, or Turkish, appear to me no other than human inventions set up to terrify and enslave mankind, and monopolize power and profit.

Age of Reason, I, 1794

Every national church or religion has established itself by pretending some special mission from God communicated to certain individuals. The Jews have their Moses; the Christians their Jesus Christ, their apostles, and saints; and the Turks their Mahomet; as if the way to God was not open to every man alike.

Age of Reason, I, 1794

Religious Freedom

❧ ☙

Spiritual freedom is the root of political liberty. . . . As the union between spiritual freedom and political liberty seems nearly inseparable, it is our duty to defend both.

Thoughts on Defensive War, 1775

As to religion, I hold it to be the indispensable duty of all government, to protect all conscientious professors thereof, and I know of no other business which government hath to do therewith.

Common Sense, 1776

Of all the tyrannies that afflict mankind, tyranny in religion is the worst. Every other species of tyranny is limited to the world we live in, but this attempts a stride beyond the grave and seeks to pursue us into eternity. It is there and not here, it is to God and not to man, it is to a heavenly and not an earthly tribunal that we are to account for our belief.

A Letter to Mr. Erskine, 1797

Religion is a private affair between every man and his Maker, and no tribunal or third party has a right to interfere between them. It is not properly a thing of this world; it is only practiced in this world; but its object is in a future world; and it is not otherwise an object of just laws than for the purpose of protecting the equal rights of all, however various their belief may be.

A Letter to Mr. Erskine, 1797

Every sectary, except the Quakers, has been a persecutor. Those who fled from persecution persecuted in their turn, and it is this confusion of creeds that has filled the world with persecution and deluged it with blood.

To Samuel Adams, Washington, January 1, 1803

Remoteness

Distance of time defaces the conception, and changes the severest sorrows into conversable amusement.

The Crisis, 1780

Like fire at a distance, you heard not even the cry; you felt not the danger, you saw not the confusion. To you every thing has been foreign.

The Crisis, 1780

Reproach

It is always painful to reproach those one would wish to respect.

To George Washington, February 22, 1795

Republican Form of Government

A Republican form of government is pointed out by nature—Kingly governments by an unequality of power. In Republican governments, the leaders of the people, if improper, are removable by vote; Kings only by arms; an unsuccessful vote in the first case, leaves the voter safe; but an unsuccessful attempt in the latter, is death.

The Forester's Letters, 1776

A Republican government hath more true grandeur in it than a Kingly one: On the part of the public it is more consistent with freemen to appoint their rulers than to have them born; and on the part of those who preside, it is far nobler to be a ruler by the choice of the people, than a King by the chance of birth. Every honest Delegate is more than a Monarch.

The Forester's Letters, 1776

All men are Republicans by nature and Royalists only by fashion.

The Forester's Letters, 1776

The republican form and principle leaves no room for insurrection, because it provides and establishes a rightful means in its stead.

Dissertations on Government, 1786

Government in a well constituted republic, requires no belief from man beyond what his reason can give. He sees the *rationale* of the whole system, its origin and its operation; and as it is best supported when best understood, the human faculties act with boldness, and acquire, under this form of Government, a gigantic manliness.

Rights of Man, I, 1791

I am a citizen of a country which knows no other majesty than that of the people—no other government than that of the representative body—no other sovereignty than that of the laws.

To the Authors of "The Republicans," 1791

Republican government is no other than government established and conducted for the interest of the public, as well individually as collectively.

Rights of Man, II, 1792

Such is the nature of representative government, that it quietly decides all matters by majority.

Rights of Man, II, 1792

The true system of Government consists, not in Kings, but in fair and honorable Representation.

Speech to the French National Convention, January 15, 1793

The true and only basis of representative government is equality of rights. Every man has a right to one vote, and no more in the choice of representatives.

Dissertation on First Principles of Government, 1795

The conviction that government, by representation, is the true system of government, is spreading itself fast in the world. The reasonableness of it can be seen by all. The justness of it makes itself felt even by its opposers.

Agrarian Justice, 1797

A republic must not only be so in its principles but in its form.

To the Citizens of the United States, 1802

The representative system is fatal to ambition.

To the Citizens of the United States, 1802

Republican Virtue

❧ ❧

When republican virtue fails, slavery ensues.

Common Sense, 1776

Reputation

❧ ❧

He who survives his reputation, lives out of spite to himself, like a man listening to his own reproach.

The American Crisis, 1778

A man may write himself out of reputation when nobody else can do it.

Rights of Man, II, 1792

Resolution

✣

Resolution is our inherent character, and courage hath never yet forsaken us.

Common Sense, 1776

Responses

✣

What they [i.e., the public] do think worth while to read, is not worth mine to answer.

Rights of Man, II, 1792

Retaliation

✣

Repeated aggravation will provoke a retort, and policy justify the measure.

The Crisis, 1778

Be assured of this, that the instant you put a threat in execution, a counter blow will follow . . . if nothing but distress can recover you to reason, to punish will become an office of charity.

The Crisis, 1778

The doctrine of not retaliating injuries is much better expressed in Proverbs, which is a collection as well from the Gentiles as the Jews, than it is in the testament. It is there said, Proverbs, xxiv, ver. 21, *If thine enemy be hungry give him bread to eat, and if he be thirsty give him water to drink.* But when it is said, as in the testament, *if a man smite thee on the right check, turn to him the other also;* it is assassinating the dignity of forbearance and sinking man into a spaniel.

Age of Reason, II, 1795

It is incumbent on man as a moralist that he does not revenge an injury; and it is equally as good in a political sense; for there is no end to retaliation; each retaliates on the other, and calls it justice.

Age of Reason, II, 1795

Retirement

❦

I live with that retirement and quiet that suits me.

To John Fellows, July 31, 1805

Revenge

❦

Men read by way of revenge.

Common Sense, 1776

Revolutions

❦

A Share in two revolutions is living to some purpose.

To George Washington, London, October 16, 1789

I have not the least doubt of the final and complete success of the French Revolution—Little Ebbings and flowings, for and against, the natural companions of revolutions, sometimes appear, but the full current of it, is, in my opinion, as fixed as the Gulf Stream.

To George Washington, London, May 1, 1790

It is perhaps impossible in the first steps which are made in a Revolution, to avoid all kind of error, in Principle or in Practice, or in some instances to prevent the Combination of both.

To the Authors of "The Republicans," 1791

I am well aware that the moment of any great change . . . is unavoidably the moment of terror and confusion. The mind, highly agitated by hope, suspicion, and apprehension, continues without rest till the change be accomplished.

Letter to the People of France, 1792

It appears to general observation, that revolutions create genius and talents; but those events do no more than bring them forward. There is existing in man, a mass of sense lying in a dormant state, and which, unless something excites it to action, will descend with him, in that condition to the grave.

Rights of Man, II, 1792

Revolutions have for their object, a change in the moral condition of governments.

Rights of Man, II, 1792

The greatest forces that can be brought into the field of revolutions, are reason and common interest. Where these can have the opportunity of acting, opposition dies with fear, or crumbles away by conviction.

Age of Reason, I, 1794

If you subvert the basis of the revolution, if you dispense with principles and substitute expedients, you will extinguish that enthusiasm and energy which have hitherto been the life and soul of the revolution; and you will substitute in its place nothing but a cold indifference and self-interest, which will again degenerate into intrigue, cunning and effeminacy.

Speech to the French National Convention, 1795

It is never to be expected in a revolution, that every man is to change his opinion at the same moment. There never yet was any truth or any principle so irresistibly obvious, that all men believed it at once. Time and reason must co-operate with each other to the final establishment of any principle; and, therefore, those who may happen to be first convinced have not a right to persecute others, on whom conviction operates more slowly. The moral principle of revolution is to instruct, not to destroy.

Dissertation on First Principles of Government, 1795

In the commencement of a revolution, the revolutionary party permit to themselves a discretionary exercise of power regulated not by circumstances than by principle, which, were the practice to continue, liberty would never be established, or if established would soon be overthrown. It is never to be expected in a revolution that every man is to change his opinion at the same moment.

Dissertation on First Principles of Government, 1795

Let us . . . do honor to revolutions by justice, and give currency to their principles by blessings.

Agrarian Justice, 1797

The time during which a revolution is proceeding is not the time when its resulting advantages can be enjoyed.

Agrarian Justice, 1797

It is the *hazard* and not the principles of a revolution that retards their progress.

Agrarian Justice, 1797

A revolution in the state of civilization, is the necessary companion of revolutions in the system of government.

Agrarian Justice, 1797

Revolutions in Thought

We see with other eyes; we hear with other ears; and think with other thoughts, than those we formerly used. We can look back on our own prejudices, as if they had been the prejudices of other people.

Letter to the Abbé Raynal, 1782

The danger to which the success of revolutions is most exposed, is that of attempting them before the principles on which they proceed, and the advantages to result from them, are sufficiently seen and understood.

Rights of Man, II, 1792

Rewards

%

My reward existed in the ambition to do good, and the independent happiness of my own mind.

To the Citizens of the United States, 1802

Right Ideas

%

The furnishing ourselves with right ideas, and the accustoming ourselves to right habits of thinking, have a powerful effect in strengthening and cementing the mind of the country and freeing it from the danger of partial or mistaken notions.

The Necessity of Taxation, 1782

Rights

%

A right, to be truly so, must be right in itself.

Public Good, 1780

The rights of men in society, are neither devisable, nor transferable, nor annihilable, but are descendable only; and it is not in the power of any generation to intercept finally, and cut off the descent.

Rights of Man, I, 1791

The natural, civil and political *rights of man* are liberty, equality, security, property, social guarantees, and resistance to oppression.

Plan of a Declaration of Rights, 1792

Rights are not *gifts* from one man to another, nor from one class of men to another; for who is he who could be the first giver, or by what principle, or on what authority could he possess the right of giving?

Dissertation on First Principles of Government, 1795

Where the rights of men are equal, every man must finally see the necessity of protecting the rights of others as the most effectual security for his own.

Dissertation on First Principles of Government, 1795

Rights of Minors

The rights of minors are as sacred as the rights of the aged.

Dissertation on First Principles of Government, 1795

Rogues

That men never turn rogues without turning fools, is a maxim, sooner or later, universally true.

The American Crisis, 1777

Rotation in Office

Never invest power long in the hands of any number of individuals. The inconveniences that may be supposed to accompany frequent changes are less to be feared than the dangers that arise from long continuance.

Dissertation on First Principles of Government, 1795

Rules

❦

Any rule which can be agreed on is better than none.

Public Good, 1780

Satire

❦

The connection between vice and meanness is a fit object for satire, but when the satire is a fact, it cuts with the irresistible power of a diamond.

The American Crisis, 1777

Science

❦

The human mind has a natural disposition to scientific knowledge, and to the things connected with it. The first and favorite amusement of a child, even before it begins to play, is that of imitating the works of man. It builds houses with cards or sticks; it navigates the little ocean of a bowl of water with a paper boat; or dams the stream of a gutter, and contrives something which it calls a mill; and it interests itself in the fate of its works with a care that resembles affection. It afterwards goes to school, where its genius is killed by the barren study of a dead language, and the philosopher is lost in the linguist.

Age of Reason, I, 1794

Every science has for its basis a system of principles as fixed and unalterable as those by which the universe is regulated and governed. Man cannot make principles; he can only discover them.

Age of Reason, I, 1794

Scientific Principles

❧ ❧

Man cannot invent any thing that is eternal and immutable; and the scientific principles he employs for this purpose, must, and are, of necessity, as eternal and immutable as the laws by which the heavenly bodies move, or they could not be used as they are, to ascertain the time when, and the manner how, an eclipse will take place.

The scientific principles that man employs to obtain the fore-knowledge of an eclipse, or of any thing else relating to the motion of the heavenly bodies, are contained chiefly in that part of science that is called trigonometry, or the properties of a triangle, which, when applied to the study of the heavenly bodies, is called astronomy; when applied to direct the course of a ship on the ocean, it is called navigation; when applied to the construction of figures drawn by a rule and compass, it is called geometry; when applied to the construction of plans of edifices, it is called architecture; when applied to the measurement of any portion of the surface of the earth, it is called land-surveying. In fine, it is the soul of science. It is an eternal truth: it contains the *mathematical demonstration* of which man speaks, and the extent of its uses are unknown.

It may be said, that man can make or draw a triangle, and therefore a triangle is an human invention.

But the triangle, when drawn, is no other than the image of the principle: it is a delineation to the eye, and from thence to the mind, of a principle that would otherwise be imperceptible. The triangle does not make the principle, any more than a candle taken into a room that was dark, makes the chairs and tables that before were invisible. All the properties of a triangle exist independently of the figure, and existed before any triangle was drawn or thought of by man. Man had no more to do in the formation of those properties, or principles, than he had to do in making the laws by which the heavenly bodies move; and therefore the one must have the same divine origin as the other. . . .

Since then man cannot make principles, from whence did he gain a knowledge of them, so as to be able to apply them, not only to things on earth, but to ascertain the motion of bodies so immensely distant from him as all the heavenly bodies are? From whence, I ask, *could* he gain that knowledge, but from the study of the true theology?

Age of Reason, I, 1794

Scripture

❧❦

The word of God cannot exist in any written or human language.

The continually progressive change to which the meaning of words is subject, the want of an universal language which renders translations necessary, the errors to which translations are again subject, the mistakes of copyists and printers, together with the possibility of willful alteration, are of themselves evidences, that human language, whether in speech or in print, cannot be the vehicle of the word of God.

Age of Reason, I, 1794

The word of God is the creation we behold. And it is in *this word*, which no human invention can counterfeit or alter, that God speaketh universally to man.

Age of Reason, I, 1794

It is only in the CREATION that all our ideas and conceptions of a *word of God* can unite.

Age of Reason, I, 1794

But though, speaking for myself, I thus admit the possibility of revelation, I totally disbelieve that the Almighty ever did communicate any thing to man by any mode of speech in any language, or by any kind of vision or appearance, or by any means which our senses are capable of receiving; otherwise than by the universal display of himself in the works of the creation, and by that repugnance we feel in ourselves to bad actions, and disposition to good ones.

Age of Reason, II, 1795

Seafaring

❦

A maritime life is a kind of partial emigration.

To Binny and Ronaldson, April 18, 1807

Secrets

❦

Nations can have no secrets, and the secrets of courts, like those of individuals, are always their defects.

Rights of Man, II, 1792

Security

❦

No country can be defended without expence.

Public Good, 1780

Common interest produces common security.

Rights of Man, II, 1792

Self-Determination

Every nation has at all times an inherent indefeasible right to constitute and establish such government for itself as best accords with its disposition, interest, and happiness.

Address and Declaration, 1791

Every nation, for the time being, has a right to govern itself as it pleases.

Dissertation on First Principles of Government, 1795

Self-Evident Truths

There are some truths so self evident and obvious . . . that they ought never to be stated in the form of a question for debate, because it is habituating the mind to think doubtfully, of what there ought to be no doubt upon.

A Friend to Rhode-Island and the Union, 1783

Self-Fulfilling Prophesies

As a man predicts ill he becomes inclined to wish it.

Age of Reason, II, 1795

Self-Interest

❧ ❧

Where nature and interest reinforce each other, the compact is too intimate to be dissolved.

The Crisis, 1780

A man's judgment in his own behalf . . . is very likely to be wrong, and between the apprehensions of saying too little, or too much, he probably errs in both.

To George Washington, October 2, 1783

Self-Preservation

❧ ❧

The supreme of all laws, in all cases, is that of self-preservation.

To the People of France and the French Armies, 1797

Self-Respect

❧ ❧

Self-respect is the attribute of a free nation, and that, when the cause which it upholds is just and glorious, it will never allow that cause to be degraded.

A Republican Manifesto, 1791

Sexual Excess

✒ ✒

Seven hundred wives, and three hundred concubines, are worse than none; and however it may carry with it the appearance of heightened enjoyment, it defeats all the felicity of affection, by leaving it no point to fix upon.

Age of Reason, II, 1795

Sharing Burdens

✒ ✒

It is not the weight of a thing, but the numbers who are to bear that weight, that makes it feel light or heavy to the shoulders of those who bear it.

To the People of France and the French Armies, 1797

Shipbuilding

✒ ✒

Shipbuilding is America's greatest pride, and in which, she will in time excel the whole world.

Common Sense, 1776

Shortness of Life

✒ ✒

Life is sufficiently short without shakng the sand that measures it.

The American Crisis, 1778

Silence

Ceremony, and even, silence, from whatever motive they may arise, have a hurtful tendency, when they give the least degree of countenance to base and wicked performances.

Common Sense, 1776

Silence becomes a kind of crime when it operates as a cover or an encouragement to the guilty.

Pennsylvania Packet, January 23, 1779

There are cases in which silence is a loud language.

To George Washington, August 3, 1796

Least said is soonest mended, and nothing said requires no mending.

To Thomas Jefferson, September 9, 1788; *Remarks on Gouverneur Morris'
Funeral Oration on Alexander Hamilton*, 1804

Simplicity

The more simple any thing is, the less liable it is to be disordered, and the easier repaired when disordered.

Common Sense, 1776

Slander

Slander belongs to the class of dastardly vices. It always acts under cover. It puts insinuation in the place of evidence, and tries to impede by pretending to believe. Its loudest language, when it speaks, is a whisper. At other times, it disguises itself in anonymous paragraphs, for which nobody is accountable.

To Mr. Hulbert of Sheffield, Mass., 1805

Slander and hypocrisy are classmates in the school of vice. They are the necessary aids of each other. The same cowardly depravity of heart that leads to the one conducts to the other.

To Mr. Hulbert of Sheffield, Mass., 1805

Slavery

If the present generation, or any other, are disposed to be slaves, it does not lessen the right of the succeeding generation to be free.

Rights of Man, I, 1791

Slavery consists in being subject to the will of another.

Dissertation on First Principles of Government, 1795

The mind bowed down by slavery loses in silence its elastic powers.

Dissertation on First Principles of Government, 1795

Smuggling

An illicit Trade, under any shape it can be placed, cannot be carried on without a violation of truth.

Commerce with Britain and the Necessity of Union, 1783

Society Versus Government

❦

Some writers have so confounded society with government, as to leave little or no distinction between them; whereas they are not only different, but have as different origins. Society is produced by our wants, and government by our wickedness; the former promotes our happiness positively by uniting our affections, the latter negatively by restraining our vices. The one encourages intercourse, the other creates distinctions. The first is a patron, the last a punisher.

Society in every state is a blessing, but government even in its best state is but a necessary evil; in its worst state an intolerable one.

Common Sense, 1776

Necessity, like a gravitating power, would soon form . . . society.

Common Sense, 1776

Great part of that order which reigns among mankind is not the effect of government. It has its origin in the principles of society and the natural constitution of man. It existed prior to government, and would exist if the formality of government was abolished. The mutual dependence and reciprocal interest which man has upon each other, create that great chain of connection which holds it together.

Rights of Man, II, 1792

Society performs for itself almost every thing which is ascribed to government.

Rights of Man, II, 1792

No one man is capable, without the aid of society, of supplying his own wants; and those wants, acting upon every individual, impel the whole of them into society, as naturally as gravitation acts to a center.

Rights of Man, II, 1792

She [i.e., nature] has not only forced man into society, by a diversity of wants, which the reciprocal aid of each other can supply, but she has implanted in him a system of social affections, which, though not necessary to his existence, are essential to his happiness. There is no period in life when this love for society ceases to act. It begins and ends with our being.

Rights of Man, II, 1792

Sovereignty

Individuals or individual states may call themselves what they please; but the world, and especially the world of enemies, is not to be held in awe by the whistling of a name. Sovereignty must have power to protect all the parts that compose and constitute it.

The Crisis, 1783

The people in America are the fountain of power.

Dissertations on Government, 1786

Sovereignty, as a matter of right, appertains to the Nation only, and not to any individual; and a Nation has at all times an inherent indefeasible right to abolish any form of Government it finds inconvenient, and establish such as accords with its interest, disposition, and happiness.

Rights of Man, I, 1791

Stability

It is not length of time, but power that gives stability.

Letter to the Abbé Raynal, 1782

State of Nature

❦

The earth, in its natural uncultivated state, was, and ever would have continued to be, the COMMON PROPERTY OF THE HUMAN RACE. In that state every man would have been born to property. He would have been a joint life-proprietor with the rest in the property of the soil, and in all its natural productions, vegetables and animal.

Agrarian Justice, 1797

Staying the Course

❦

We have at present steered with safety through a rough sea, and are bringing the ship into port, let us take care she is not shipwreck'd in the harbor.

The Crisis, 1778

Stories

❦

Almost all romantic stories have been suggested by some actual circumstance.

Age of Reason, II, 1795

Strange Bedfellows

Parties directly opposite in principle will sometimes concur in pushing forward the same movement with very different views, and with the hopes of its producing very different consequences.

Rights of Man, I, 1791

Study

My study is to be useful.

The American Crisis, 1777

Sublime

One step above the sublime makes the ridiculous, and one step above the ridiculous makes the sublime again.

Age of Reason, I, 1794

Submission

Submission is wholly a vassalage term, repugnant to the dignity of Freedom, and an echo of the language used at the Conquest.

Rights of Man, I, 1791

Sudden Changes

※⟨⟩※

There are but few instances, in which the mind is fitted for sudden transitions; it takes in its pleasures by reflection and comparison, and those must have time to act, before the relish for new scenes is complete.

The Crisis, 1783

Suffrage

※⟨⟩※

The right of voting for representatives is the primary right by which other rights are protected.

Dissertation on First Principles of Government, 1795

To deprive half the people in a nation of their rights as citizens is an easy matter in theory or on paper, but it is a most dangerous experiment, and rarely practicable in the execution.

Speech to the French National Convention, 1795

Let us maintain inviolably equality in the sacred right of suffrage: public security can never have a basis more solid. *Salut et Fraternite.*

Agrarian Justice, 1797

The silent vote, or the simple *yea or nay*, is more powerful than the bayonet, and decides the strength of numbers without a blow.

To the Citizens of Pennsylvania on the Proposal for Calling a Convention, 1805

Suggestions

❦

Could the straggling thoughts of individuals be collected, they would frequently form materials for wise and able men to improve into useful matter.

Common Sense, 1776

Suitability

❦

Nature, in the arrangement of mankind, has fitted some for every service in life. Were all soldiers, all would starve and go naked, and were none soldiers, all would be slaves.

The American Crisis, 1777

Supposition

❦

Supposition proves nothing.

Age of Reason, II, 1795

Surprise

❦

We may be surprised by events we did not expect.

The American Crisis, 1777

Suspicion

❧ ☙

Suspicion is the companion of mean souls, and the bane of all good society.

Common Sense, 1776

Suspicion and persecution are weeds of the same dunghill, and flourish best together.

The American Crisis, 1777

Suspicion may be spread without any trouble; it cannot be uprooted with anything like the same facility. If you try to eradicate it forcibly, you fail; but if you succeed in quietly undermining it, it will gradually pass away silently and noiselessly.

Answers to Four Questions on Legislative and Executive Powers, 1791

I am not of a disposition inclined to suspicion. It is in its nature a mean and cowardly passion, and upon the whole, even admitting error into the case, it is better, I am sure it is more generous, to be wrong on the side of confidence than on the side of suspicion.

To Samuel Adams, Washington, January 1, 1803

Sympathy

❧ ☙

What renders us kind and humane? Is it not sympathy, the power which I have of putting myself in my neighbor's place?

An Essay for the Use of New Republicans, 1792

Talents

❧ ❧

Talents and abilities cannot have hereditary descent.

Rights of Man, I, 1791

Tariff

❧ ❧

There are many reasons why a duty on imports is the most convenient duty or tax that can be collected, one of which is, because the whole is payable in a few places in a country, and it likewise operates with the greatest ease and equality, because as every one pays in proportion to what he consumes, so people in general consume in proportion to what they can afford, and therefore the tax is regulated by the abilities which every man supposes himself to have, or in other words every man becomes his own assessor, and pays by a little at a time when it suits him to buy. Besides, it is a tax which people may pay or let alone by not consuming the articles; and though the alternative may have no influence on their conduct, the power of choosing is an agreeable thing to the mind.

The Crisis Extraordinary, 1780

Taxes

❧ ❧

Taxation . . . could never be worth the charge of obtaining it by arms.

The Crisis, 1778

No country can be defended without expense.

Public Good, 1780

It is impossible to compel the payment of taxes by force, when a whole nation is determined to take its stand upon that ground.

Rights of Man, I, 1791

If taxes are necessary, they are of course advantageous; but if they require an apology, the apology itself implies an impeachment.

Rights of Man, I, 1791

We still find the greedy hand of government thrusting itself into every corner and crevice of industry, and grasping the spoil of the multitude. Invention is continually exercised, to furnish new presences for revenue and taxation. It watches prosperity as its prey, and permits none to escape without a tribute.

Rights of Man, II, 1792

It is a general idea, that when taxes are once laid on, they are never taken off.

Rights of Man, II, 1792

Temper

❧⚘

Sudden transitions of temper are seldom lasting.

Common Sense, 1776

A man may easily distinguish in himself between temper and principle.

The American Crisis, 1776

Theology

❧⚘

The study of theology in books of opinions has often produced fanaticism, rancor and cruelty of temper; and from hence have proceeded the numerous persecutions, the fanatical quarrels, the religious burnings and massacres, that have desolated Europe.

A Discourse at the Society of Theophilanthropists, 1797

Thinking

❦

For the want of leisure to think, we unavoidably wasted knowledge.

The American Crisis, 1777

Thinking Alike

❦

People, however remote, who think alike will unavoidable speak alike.

The Crisis, 1782

Thoughts

❦

I have often observed that by lending words for my thoughts I understand my thoughts the better. Thoughts are a kind of mental smoke, which require words to illuminate them.

To Benjamin Franklin, December 31, 1785

There are two distinct classes of what we call Thoughts: those that we produce in ourselves by reflection and the act of thinking, and those that bolt into the mind of their own accord. I have always made it a rule to treat those voluntary visitors with civility, taking care to examine, as well as I was able, if they were worth entertaining; and it is from them I have acquired almost all the knowledge that I have.

Age of Reason, I, 1794

Who can say by what exceeding fine action of fine matter it is, that a thought is produced in what we call the mind; and yet that thought, when produced, as I now produce the thought I am writing, is capable of becoming immortal, and is the only production of man that has that capacity. Statues of brass or marble will perish, and statues made in imitation of them are not the same statues, nor the same workmanship, any more than a copy of a picture is the same picture. But print and reprint a thought a thousand times over, and that, with materials of any kind, carve it in wood, or engrave it in stone, the thought is eternally and identically the same thought in every case. It has a capacity of unimpaired existence, unaffected by change of matter, and is essentially distinct, and of a nature different, from every thing else that we know of, or can conceive.

Age of Reason, II, 1795

Let but a single idea begin and a thousand will soon follow.

Dissertation on First Principles of Government, 1795

Time

❧ ☙

Time makes more converts than reason.

Common Sense, 1776

Interest and Time have an amazing influence over the understanding of mankind, and reconcile them to almost every species of absurdity and injustice.

Four Letters on Interesting Subjects, 1776

It is difficult beyond the power of man to conceive an eternal duration of what we call time; but it is more impossible to conceive a time when there shall be no time.

Age of Reason, I, 1794

Time and Principles

❦

Time with respect to principles is an eternal NOW: it has no operation upon them: it changes nothing of their nature and qualities. But what have we to do with a thousand years? Our lifetime is but a short portion of that period, and if we find the wrong in existence as soon as we begin to live, that is the point of time at which it begins to us; and our right to resist it is the same as if it never existed before.

Dissertation on First Principles of Government, 1795

Titles

❦

But if we proceed on [into antiquity], we shall come to the time when man came from the hand of his Maker. What was he then? Man. Man was his high and only title, and a higher cannot be given him.

Rights of Man, I, 1791

Titles are but nick-names, and every nick-name is a title. The thing is perfectly harmless in itself, but it marks a sort of foppery in the human character which degrades it.

Rights of Man, I, 1791

Tolerance

❦

Between Men in pursuit of truth, and whose object is the happiness of Man both here and hereafter, there ought to be no reserve. Even Error has a claim to indulgence, if not to respect, when it is believed to be truth.

To Samuel Adams, Washington, January 1, 1803

Toleration

✍

Toleration is not the *opposite* of Intoleration, but is the *counterfeit* of it. Both are despotisms. The one assumes to itself the right of with-holding Liberty of Conscience, and the other of granting it. The one is the pope, armed with fire and faggot, and the other is the pope selling or granting indulgences. The former is church and state, and the latter is church and traffic.

But Toleration may be viewed in a much stronger light. Man wor-ships not himself, but his Maker; and the liberty of conscience which he claims, is not for the service of himself, but of his God. In this case, therefore, we must necessarily have the associated idea of two beings; the *mortal* who renders the worship, and the IMMORTAL BEING who is worshipped. Toleration, therefore, places itself, not between man and man, nor between church and church, nor between denom-ination of religion and another, but between God and man; between the being who worships, and the BEING who is worshipped; and by the same act of assumed authority by which it tolerates man to pay his worship, it presumptuously and blasphemously sets itself up to toler-ate the Almighty to receive it.

Rights of Man, I, 1791

Trade

✍

Trade flourishes best when it is free, and it is weak policy to attempt to fetter it.

The Crisis, 1778

Treachery

❧

Conquest may be effected under the pretense of friendship.

Common Sense, 1776

To live beneath the authority of those whom we cannot love, is misery, slavery, or what name you please. In that case, there will never be peace. Security will be a thing unknown, because, a treacherous friend in power, is the most dangerous of enemies.

The Forester's Letters, 1776

Treason

❧

A traitor is the foulest fiend on earth!

The American Crisis, 1777

Treaties

❧

There is nothing sets the character of a nation in a higher or lower light with others, than the faithfully fulfilling, or perfidiously breaking of treaties. They are things not to be tampered with.

The Crisis, 1782

Treaties of Peace

❦

Peace, by treaty, is only a cessation of violence, not a reformation of sentiment.

The Crisis, 1778

Truth

❦

Truths discovered by necessity, will appear clearer and stronger every day.

Common Sense, 1776

Truth, in every case, is the most reputable victory a man can gain.

Pennsylvania Packet, February 16, 1779

It is by thinking upon and talking Subjects over that we approach truth.

To Thomas Jefferson, September 28, 1790

The graceful pride of truth knows no extremes, and preserves, in every latitude of life, the right-angled character of man.

Rights of Man, I, 1791

Such is the irresistible nature of truth, that all it asks, and all it wants, is the liberty of appearing. The sun needs no inscription to distinguish him from darkness.

Rights of Man, II, 1792

Truth, whenever it can fully appear, is a thing so naturally familiar to the mind, that an acquaintance commences at first sight. No artificial light, yet discovered, can display all the properties of daylight; so neither can the best invented fiction fill the mind with every conviction which truth begets.

Letter Addressed to the Addressers, 1792

Mystery is the antagonist of truth. It is a fog of human invention that obscures truth, and represents it in distortion.

Age of Reason, I, 1794

Truth is an uniform thing.

Age of Reason, II, 1795

When opinions are free, either in matters of government or religion, truth will finally and powerfully prevail.

Age of Reason, II, 1795

There is a general and striking difference between the genuine effects of truth itself, and the effects of falsehoods believed to be truth. Truth is naturally benign; but falsehood believed to be truth is always furious. The former delights in serenity, is mild and persuasive, and seeks not the auxiliary aid of invention. The latter sticks at nothing. It has naturally no morals. Every lie is welcome that suits its purpose. It is the innate character of the thing, to act in this manner, and the criterion by which it may be known, whether in politics or religion.

To the Citizens of the United States, 1802

Types of Men

%℃ ℋ

There are three sorts of men in every State, the willing and able, the willing and not able, and the able and *not* willing.

Serious Address to the People of Pennsylvania, 1778

Tyranny

%℃ ℋ

Tyranny, like hell, is not easily conquered; yet we have this consolation with us, that the harder the conflict, the more glorious the triumph.

What we obtain too cheap, we esteem too lightly:—'Tis dearness only that gives every thing its value.

The American Crisis, 1776

Unicameralism

❧ ☙

A single legislature, into the hands of whatever party it may fall, is capable of being made a complete aristocracy for the time it exists.

On the Affairs of Pennsylvania, 1786

A single legislature, on account of the superabundance of its power, and the uncontrolled rapidity of its execution, becomes as dangerous to the principles of liberty as that of a despotic monarchy.

On the Affairs of Pennsylvania, 1786

Union

❧ ☙

. . . the Union of the States. On this, our great national character depends. It is this which must give us importance abroad and security at home. It is through this only that we are, or can be nationally known in the world.

The Crisis, 1783

Unity

❧ ☙

It is not in numbers, but in unity, that our great strength lies.

Common Sense, 1776

Mutual fear is a principal link in the chain of mutual love.

The American Crisis, 1776

The Universe

%%%

It is difficult beyond description to conceive that space can have no end; but it is more difficult to conceive an end.

Age of Reason, I, 1794

It is from the study of the true theology that all our knowledge of science is derived, and it is from that knowledge that all the arts have originated.

The Almighty lecturer, by displaying the principles of science in the structure of the universe, has invited man to study and to imitation. It is as if he had said to the inhabitants of this globe that we call ours, "I have made an earth for man to dwell upon, and I have rendered the starry heavens visible, to teach him science and the arts. He can now provide for his own comfort, AND LEARN FROM MY MUNIFICENCE TO ALL, TO BE KIND TO EACH OTHER."

Of what use is it, unless it be to teach man something, that his eye is endowed with the power of beholding, to an incomprehensible distance, an immensity or worlds revolving in the ocean of space? Or of what use is it that this immensity of worlds is visible to man? What has man to do with the Pleides, with Orion, with Sirius, with the star he calls the north star, with the moving orbs he has named Saturn, Jupiter, Mars, Venus, and Mercury, if no uses are to follow from their being visible? A less power of vision would have been sufficient for man, if the immensity he now possesses were given only to waste itself, as it were, on an immense desert of space glittering with shows.

It is only by contemplating what he calls the starry heavens, as the book and school of science, that he discovers any use in their being visible to him, or any advantage resulting from his immensity of vision. But when he contemplates from the subject in this light, he sees an additional motive for saying that *nothing was made in vain;* for in vain would be this power of vision if it taught man nothing.

The circular dimensions of our world in the widest part, as a man would measure the widest round of an apple or a ball, is only twenty five thousand and twenty English miles, reckoning sixty nine miles and an half to an equatorial degree, and may be sailed round in the space of about three years.

A world of this extent may, at first thought, appear to us to be great; but if we compare it with the immensity of space in which it is suspended, like a bubble or a balloon in the air, it is infinitely less in proportion than the smallest grain of sand is to the size of the world, or the finest particle of dew to the whole ocean; and is therefore but small; and . . . is only *one* of a system of worlds, of which the universal creation is composed.

It is not difficult to gain some faint idea of the immensity of space in which this and all the other worlds are suspended, if we follow a progression of ideas. When we think of the size of dimensions of a room, our ideas limit themselves to the walls, and there they stop. But when our eye, or our imagination, darts into space, that is, when it looks upward into what we call the open air, we cannot conceive any walls or boundaries it can have; and if for the sake of resting our ideas, we suppose a boundary, the question immediately renews itself, and asks, what is beyond that next boundary? and in the same manner, what is beyond the next boundary? and so on, till the fatigued imagination returns and says, there is no end. . . .

If we take a survey of our own world, or rather of this, of which the Creator has given us the use, as our portion in the immense system of creation, we find every part of it, the earth, the waters, and the air that surround it, filled, and, as it were crowded with life, down from the largest animals that we know of, to the smallest insects the naked eye can behold, and from thence to others still smaller, and totally invisible without the assistance of the microscope. Every tree, every plant, every leaf, serves not only as an habitation, but as a world to some numerous race, till animal existence becomes so exceedingly refined, that the effluvia of a blade of grass would be food for thousands.

Since then no part of our earth is left unoccupied, why is it to be supposed, that the immensity of space is a naked void, lying in eternal waste. There is room for millions of worlds as large or larger than ours, and each of them millions of miles apart from each other.

Age of Reason, I, 1794

Unjust Measures

❧

Unjust measures must be supported by unjust means.

To the Opposers of the Bank, 1787

Ups and Downs

❧

The tide of all human affairs has its ebbs and flow in directions contrary to each other.

Rights of Man, II, 1792

Usurpation

❧

Usurpation cannot alter the right of things.

Rights of Man, I, 1791

Valor

❧

The valor of a country may be learned by the bravery of its soldiers, and the general cast of its inhabitants.

The Crisis, 1780

Vanity

❧ ❦

If you are not great enough to have ambition you are little enough to have vanity.

To George Washington, August 3, 1796

Vice

❧ ❦

But while we give no encouragement to the importation of foreign vices, we ought to be equally careful not to create any. A vice begotten might be worse than a vice imported. The latter, depending on favor, would be a sycophant; the other, by pride of birth would be a tyrant. To the one we should be dupes, to the other slaves.

The Pennsylvania Magazine, I, 1775

Nothing but heaven is impregnable to vice.

Common Sense, 1776

It is a much pleasanter task to prevent vice than to punish it.

The American Crisis, 1777

One vice will frequently expel another without the least merit in the man, as powers in contrary directions reduce each other to rest.

The American Crisis, 1778

An association of vices will reduce us more than the sword.

The Crisis, 1780

Some vices make their approach with such a splendid appearance, that we scarcely know to what class of moral distinctions they belong. They are rather virtues corrupted than vices originally.

Meanness and ingratitude have nothing equivocal in their character. There is not a trait in them that renders them doubtful. They are so originally vicious, that they are generated in the dung of other vices, and crawl into existence with the filth upon their backs.

To George Washington, August 3, 1796

Victory

❧

Nothing is more common than to agree in the conquest and quarrel for the prize.

The American Crisis, 1778

The hope of final victory, which never left them [i.e., Americans], served to lighten the load and sweeten the cup allotted them to drink.

The Crisis, 1780

Vigor

❧

Vigor and determination will do any thing and every thing.

The American Crisis, 1778

Virtue

❧

Virtue . . . is not hereditary, neither is it perpetual.

Common Sense, 1776

Virtue is not hereditary either in the office or in the persons.

A Serious Address to the People of Pennsylvania, 1778

Volunteerism

❧

I am not tired of working for nothing but I cannot afford it.

To Thomas Jefferson, October 4, 1800

I must be in every thing what I have ever been, a disinterested volunteer; my proper sphere of action is on the common floor of citizenship, and to honest men I give my hand and my heart freely.

To the Citizens of the United States, 1802

Voting

❧

The silent vote, or the simple *yea or nay*, is more powerful than the bayonet, and decides the strength of numbers without a blow.

To the Citizens of Pennsylvania on the Proposal for Calling a Convention, 1805

War

❧

The fate of war is uncertain.

Common Sense, 1776

No going to law with nations; cannon are the barristers of Crowns; and the sword, not of justice, but of war, decides the suit.

Common Sense, 1776

The spirit of duelling, extended on a national scale, is a proper character for European wars. They have seldom any other motive than pride, or any other object than fame.

The American Crisis, 1777

If there is a sin superior to every other it is that of willful and offensive war. Most other sins are circumscribed within narrow limits, that is, the power of *one* man cannot give them a very general extension, and many kind of sins have only a mental existence from which no infection arises; but he who is the author of a war, lets loose the whole contagion of Hell, and opens a vein that bleeds a nation to death.

The American Crisis, 1778

It is the object only of war that makes it honorable.

The American Crisis, 1778

There is something in a war carried on by invasion which makes it differ in circumstances from any other mode of war, because he who conducts it cannot tell whether the ground he gains, be for him, or against him, when he first makes it. . . . And whoever will attend to the circumstances and events of a war carried on by invasion, will find, that any invader, in order to be finally conquered must first begin to conquer.

The American Crisis, 1778

In a general view there are very few conquests that repay the charge of making them, and mankind are pretty well convinced that it can never be worth their while to go to war for profit sake. If they are made war upon, their country invaded, or their existence at stake, it is their duty to defend and preserve themselves, but in every other light and from every other cause is war inglorious and detestable.

The Crisis, 1778

War never can be the interest of a trading nation, any more than quarreling can be profitable to a man of business.

The Crisis, 1778

To make war upon those who trade with us, is like setting a bulldog upon a customer at the shop door.

The Crisis, 1778

The seeds of almost every former war have been sown in the injudicious or defective terms of the preceding peace.

Peace, and the Newfoundland Fisheries, 1779

No human foresight can discern, no conclusion can be formed, what turn a war might take, if once set on foot by an invasion.

The Crisis, 1780

There are situations a nation may be in, in which peace or war, abstracted from every other consideration, may be politically right or wrong. When nothing can be lost by a war, but what must be lost without it, war is then the policy of that country. . . . But when no security can be gained by a war, but what may be accomplished by a peace, the case becomes reversed.

The Crisis, 1780

It is not among the least of the calamities of a long continued war, that it unhinges the mind from those nice sensations which at other times appear so amiable. The continual spectacle of woe blunts the finer feelings, and the necessity of bearing with the sight renders it familiar. In like manner, are many of the moral obligations of society weakened, till the custom of acting by necessity, becomes an apology where it is truly a crime.

The Crisis, 1783

War involves in its progress such a train of unforeseen and unsupposed circumstances . . . that no human wisdom can calculate the end. It has but one thing certain, and that is to increase taxes.

Prospects on the Rubicon, 1787

A country invaded is in the condition of a house broke into, and on no other principle than this, can a reflective mind at least such as mine, justify war to itself.

To the Marquis of Lansdowne, September 21, 1787

Flames once kindled are not always easily extinguished.

Prospects on the Rubicon, 1787

Man, is not the enemy of man, but through the medium of a false system of Government.

Rights of Man, I, 1791

War is the Pharo table of governments, and nations the dupes of the game.

Rights of Man, II, 1792

Man, were he not corrupted by governments, is naturally the friend of man.

Rights of Man, II, 1792

War Profiteers

That there are men in all countries to whom a state of war is a mine of wealth, is a fact never to be doubted. Characters like these naturally breed in the putrefaction of distempered times, and after fattening on the disease they perish with it, or impregnated with the stench retreat into obscurity.

The Crisis, 1780

Weakness in War

But in war we may be certain of these two things, viz. that cruelty in an enemy, and motions made with more than usual parade, are always signs of weakness. He that can conquer, finds his mind too free and pleasant to be brutish; and he that intends to conquer, never makes too much show of his strength.

The American Crisis, 1777

Wealth

❧

Oppression is often the consequence, but seldom or never the means of riches.

Common Sense, 1776

The more men have to lose, the less willing are they to venture. The rich are in general slaves to fear, and submit to courtly power with the trembling duplicity of a Spaniel.

Common Sense, 1776

It is not the number of dollars a man has, but how far they will go, that makes him either rich or poor.

The American Crisis, 1777

Wealth is often the presumptive evidence of dishonesty; and poverty the negative evidence of innocence.

Dissertation on First Principles of Government, 1795

It is wrong to say God made *rich* and *poor*; He made only *male* and *female*; and He gave them the earth for their inheritance.

Agrarian Justice, 1797

The contrast of affluence and wretchedness continually meeting and offending the eye, is like dead and living bodies chained together. Though I care as little about riches as any man, I am a friend to riches because they are capable of good.

I care not how affluent some may be, provided that none be miserable in consequence of it. But it is impossible to enjoy affluence with the felicity it is capable of being enjoyed, while so much misery is mingled in the scene. The sight of the misery, and the unpleasant sensations it suggests, which, though they may be suffocated cannot be extinguished, are a greater drawback upon the felicity of affluence than the proposed 10 percent [inheritance tax] upon property is worth. He that would not give the one to get rid of the other, has no charity, even for himself.

Agrarian Justice, 1797

Weapons

❧

The supposed quietude of a good man allures the ruffian; while on the other hand, arms like laws discourage and keep the invader and the plunderer in awe, and preserve order in the world as well as property.

Thoughts on Defensive War, 1775

Wisdom

❧

Wisdom cannot be all on one side, nor ignorance all on the other.

Four Letters on Interesting Subjects, 1776

Wisdom is not the purchase of a day.

The American Crisis, 1776

It is impossible to make wisdom hereditary.

Rights of Man, I, 1791

Whatever wisdom constituently is, it is like a seedless plant; it may be reared when it appears, but it cannot be voluntarily produced. There is always a sufficiency somewhere in the general mass of society for all purposes; but with respect to the parts of society, it is continually changing its place. It rises in one today, in another tomorrow, and has most probably visited in rotation every family of the earth, and again withdrawn.

Rights of Man, II, 1792

Wisdom does not consist in the mere knowledge of language, but of things.

To Gilbert Wakefield, November 19, 1795

Wishes

❧ ❧

It is easier to wish than to obtain the object wished for, and we readily resolve on what is afterwards difficult to execute.

To Daniel Clymer, September 1786

Wit

❧ ❧

Wit is naturally a volunteer, delights in action, and under proper discipline is capable of great execution.

The Pennsylvania Magazine, I, 1775

Women

❧ ❧

If we take a survey of ages and of countries, we shall find the women, almost—without exception—at all times and in all places, adored and oppressed. Man, who has never neglected an opportunity of exerting his power, in paying homage to their beauty, has always availed himself of their weakness. He has been at once their tyrant and their slave.

An Occasional Letter on the Female Sex, 1775

Writers

Universal empire is the prerogative of a writer. His concerns are with all mankind, and though he cannot command their obedience, he can assign them their duty.

The American Crisis, 1777

Writing

What I write is pure nature, and my pen and my soul have ever gone together.

The American Crisis, 1777

To fit the powers of thinking and the turn of language to the subject, so as to bring out a clear conclusion that shall hit the point in question and nothing else, is the true criterion of writing.

Letter to the Abbé Raynal, 1782

Wrong and Right

The wrong which began a thousand years ago is as much a wrong as if it began today; and the right which originates today is as much a right as if it had the sanction of a thousand years.

Dissertation on First Principles of Government, 1795

Wrongs

❧ ☙

Wrongs cannot have a legal descent.

Rights of Man, I, 1791

Youth

❧ ☙

Youth is the seed time of good habits, as well in nations as in individuals.

Common Sense, 1776

Zealots

❧ ☙

Such men are never good moral evidences of any doctrine they preach. They are always in extremes, as well of action as of belief.

Age of Reason, II, 1795

Zealousness

❧ ☙

Those whose talent it is to act, are seldom much devoted to deliberate thinking; and feeling that they mean well they suppose it impossible to be wrong, and in the confidence of success overlook the trouble that lies concealed.

Pennsylvania Packet, October 16, 1779

INDEX

abilities. *See* talents

absolute power, 154. *See also* despotism; power; tyranny

accommodation, 192

action, 37

Adam, 198

Adams, Abigail, 9

Adams, John, 1, 7, 9–10, 11

Adams, Samuel, 7, 30

adaptability, 37

adversity, 37

advice, 38

Aesop's Fables, 38

Africa, 102

Age of Reason, 1

Age of Reason, 1, 27–28

agriculture, 38. *See also* farmers; farming

Aitken, Robert, 5–6

alarms, 39

altering government, 39

ambition, 39, 49, 83, 202; to do good, 207; and vanity, 237

amendments, 39, 66

America, 40; belongs to different system from England, 43; discovery of, 43; as example of freedom, 40–42; as mother church of government, 39, 42; as religious asylum, 43

American Crisis, 11, 32–33

American Revolution, 8–19, 43–45

ancestry, 45

ancients, 76, 179–80. *See also* antiquity

anger, 46

animals, cruelty to, 158

anonymous publications, 46

anti-isolationism, 46

antiquity, 41, 161, 173. *See also* ancients

apology, 56

appropriations, 47

architecture, 210

aristocracy, 47, 80, 112, 234; requires ignorance for support, 86. *See also* nobility

armies, 48, 164, 237. *See also* defense; military bearing; military command

Articles of Confederation, 14, 24

artifice, 48, 185

arts, 96; has its own language, 133; science as foundation of, 48, 51

Asia, 102

assertions, 49

astonishment, 49

astronomy, 60, 210, 235. *See also* the universe

atheism, 195

avarice, 49–50, 83, 186; phoenix of, 50. *See also* misers

Bache, Richard, 4

Bache, Sarah, 19

bad causes, 50, 152

Bank of North America, 23

Bank of Pennsylvania, 11–12, 23

bankruptcy, 4, 24, 50; character subject
    to, 57
banks, 50
Barlow, Joel, 1
Bartlett, Josiah, 9
Bastille, 24, 25, 41–42, 81. *See also*
    French Revolution
beginnings, 51, 122
beliefs, 51. *See also* creeds
benefit to society, 51
benevolence, 84. *See also* munificence;
    philanthropy
Bible, the, 10, 52; criticism of, 28, 52,
    79, 195; as foundation of all science,
    73. *See also* The Creation; God;
    religion; Scripture
bigotry, 125
bills of rights, 25, 52–53. *See also* natural
    rights; rights
blessings in disguise, 53
boundaries, 53
bravery, 37, 125, 237. *See also* courage;
    cowardice
breadth of perspective, 53–54
burdens: sharing, 215
Burke, Edmund, 24, 25, 111, 198

calmness, 55, 65
calumny, 55
candor, 64, 193
cause and effect, 55, 64
censure, 56
ceremony, 56, 216
change, 56
character, 56–58, 65, 173, 195; national,
    159; and public service, 189. *See also*
    integrity
charity, 58
Chastellux, Marquis de, 18
cheat, 64
checks and balances, 58–59
Cheetham, James, 11
children: harm done to by fables, 38;
    rights of, 208
choices, 59, 225
Christianity, 28, 59–60, 197; and Dark
    Ages, 76–77. *See also* Jesus Christ;
    religion; trinity

citizenship, 60–61, 196, 240
civil manners, 191
civil rights, 172; definition of, 161, 162,
    208; natural rights as foundation for,
    52–53, 61
civilization, 61. *See also* society versus
    government
clemency, 61
closed-mindedness, 62
closing a letter, 62
commerce, 62–63, 96, 164. *See also* trade
Common Sense: description of, 7–10;
    writing of, 6–7
common sense, 93, 191. *See also*
    judgment; prudence
comparison, 63
compassion, 63
concealment. *See* openness; secrecy
confidence, 63–64, 166
conquering armies, 48
conquest, 64, 173, 178
conscience, 44, 64, 158
conscience, liberty of, 230
consciousness of existence, 119
consequences, 64–65
consistency, 65, 183
consolation, 65
conspiracy, 65–66
constitutional amendments, 66
constitutional provisions, 67
constitutions, 25, 67–69; written by
    conventions, 42; versus government,
    67
contempt, 70
copyright, 70
correspondence, 70; closing a letter, 62
corroboration, 71
corruption, 71
courage, 71, 192, 203
courtiers, 72
covetousness, 72, 171, 189
cowardice, 44, 72. *See also* bravery;
    courage
craftiness, 188. *See also* cunning
Creation, The, 72–73, 158, 163; and
    beginning of rights, 162, 180; word
    of God as, 28, 72, 73, 107–8, 195,
    196, 211–12; man did not make the

earth, 186; Quakers would have made it drab, 190; story of and equality of man, 90

Creator: dishonored by the Bible, 52; God as, 27–28, 107, 108, 134; land is free gift of, 137. *See also* God

credit, 73. *See also* money

credulity, 74

creeds, 30, 74–75, 93

crimes of the heart, 75

crisis, 75–76

Crisis Extraordinary, The, 13, 15

cunning, 48, 76. *See also* craftiness

cure of disease, 76

curiosity, 76, 129

custom, 116. *See also* habit

Dark Ages, 76–77

Deane, Silas, 11

dearness, 77, 234

death, 77. *See also* life, shortness of

Death, William, 3

death penalty, 78

debt, 73

deception, 78

defamation, 166

defense, 78, 164, 225

deism, 79, 190, 195, 196

deists, 73, 198

deliberateness, 79

democracy, 80, 112. *See also* people, the

despair, 80

despotism, 70, 81–82, 103, 184. *See also* power; tyranny

destiny, shaping of, 82

determination, 239

diatribes, 82

Dickson, William, 28

dignity, 82

diplomats, 83

disarmament, 83. *See also* war; weapons

discretion, 193. *See also* judgment; prudence

discussion, 192

disease, cure of, 76

disgrace, 57

disobedience, 84

disorder, 84

disposition, 84, 86, 213

distress, 37, 84, 113

diversity, 85

doubt, 85

dreams, 85

Duane, James, 21–22

dueling, 240

Dumont, Etienne, 26

duty, 86, 189

earth, 236, 237. *See also* The Creation; universe

ease, 80

education, 86–87. *See also* knowledge; learning

elections, 87

ends, 87

enemies, 88, 103, 243; justice due, 135. *See also* war

England, 155; belongs to different system from U.S., 43; Constitution of, 89; form of government of, 67; loss of freedom in, 102; not parent of America, 91. *See also* Great Britain

enlightened attitudes, 89

envy, 90

equality of man, 90, 208

errors, 31, 75, 90–91, 183, 185, 205. *See also* mistake

Euclid, 121

Europe, 91, 102. *See also* England; France; French Revolution; Great Britain; Spain

events, 91

evils, 92, 152. *See also* wicked

examples, 92

expedience, 92, 205

experience, 92–93, 152

fables, 38, 93, 123

face saving, 93

factions, 93. *See also* political parties

facts, 94, 192

false optimism, 94

false testimony, 94

falsehoods, 233

fame, 47, 95, 240. *See also* popularity

fanaticism, 195, 226. *See also* zealots

farmers, 95
farming, 96. *See also* agriculture
fines, 96
fire, 200
first impressions, 96–97
first principles, 97
fear, 81
flattery, 97
follow-through, lack of, 137
folly, 97
foolish risks, 98
foolish things, 98
fools, 98
foppery, 98, 229
forbearance, 204
force, 192
foreign affairs, 99; of U.S., 42. *See also*
    commerce; diplomats; Europe;
    treaties
foreign opinion, 99
forgetfulness, 80, 84, 99
forgiveness, 129
forms of government, 68, 99, 116. *See
    also* aristocracy; democracy;
    despotism; mixed government;
    monarchy; republican form of
    government
fortitude, 40, 65, 72, 101
foundations for debate, 101
France, 8, 11–12, 15, 24. *See also*
    Bastille; French Revolution
Franklin, Benjamin, 3, 4, 7, 15, 167
Franklin, William, 4
fraud, 101–2
freedom, 102–3; America as example of,
    40–42; is happiness, 136. *See also*
    bills of rights; law of nature; liberty;
    natural rights
French Revolution, 24–27, 89, 204. *See
    also* Bastille
friendship, 46, 103–4, 117, 147–48, 231
frugality, 72
future generations, 104–5

Gallatin, Albert, 32
general consent, 192
genius: differs from judgment, 105, 134;
    killed by schooling, 209; magazines

as nursery of, 145; revolutions
    create, 205
geography, 106
geometry, 210
George III, 155, 193
Gerry, Elbridge, 22
goals, 106
God, 107–8, 230; belief in one, 30, 75,
    195; duty to, 86, 111; only thing for
    Americans to fear, 42; to be found in
    Creation, 27–28, 73, 107–8; goodness
    of, 158; men are responsible to for
    religion, 195; reason discovers, 27–28,
    107, 193; resignation to will of, 32,
    179
going the full course, 109, 220. *See also*
    perseverance
gold and silver, 109
good and bad, 109, 152
good example, 66
good opinion, 63, 159
good versus bad causes, 110
government, 110–13; altering
    government, 39; America as mother
    church of, 39, 42; confidence in,
    80; versus constitution, 67; mixed,
    153; as a natural right, 67; origin
    of, 112; people as in America, 40;
    purpose of, 100; revolution in
    principles and practice of, 45;
    versus society, 218–19. *See also*
    aristocracy; despotism; forms of
    government; laws; monarchy;
    republican form of government;
    sovereignty
government authority, 113–14
government forms, 114
gravity, 165
Great Britain: and American
    Revolution, 45; incompetence
    of, 54. *See also* England
great men, 47
great objects, 114
greatness, 114
Greeks, 41, 196
Greene, Nathanael, 11, 14, 18
grief, 91, 115
guilt: unwilling to die, 90

guilt of government, 115
gullibility, 115

habit, 115; of right thinking, 207. *See also* custom
Hamilton, Alexander, 26
Hancock, John, 8
happiness, 61, 116–17, 125, 195, 196, 207, 229; freedom is, 136; purpose of government, 100, 111, 113, 213; in hereafter, 75, 118; society promotes, 218
hardships, 117, 171
harmony, 117
hasty judgments, 117
health, 118
heaven, 30, 118, 196
hell, 118
Henry, Patrick, 22
hereafter, the, 30–31, 118–20; hope for, 75, 118. *See also* God; religion
hereditary government, 120–21. *See also* monarchy
hints, 121
history, 122–23. *See also* ancients; antiquity
honesty, 123, 168, 189, 191
hopeless situations, 124. *See also* despair
human beings, 124; movement of the body, 159; types of, 233
human nature, 124
humanity, 125, 142, 184
hypocrisy, 125–26, 183, 187, 196, 217

ideas, 126, 187. *See also* thoughts
ignorance, 113, 126, 136, 192. *See also* knowledge; wisdom
ill opinion, 127
imagination, 85, 112, 127
imitation, 66, 127
immigrants, loyalty of, 144–45
impetuosity, 128
improvement, 128
inertia, 128
infidelity, 125, 128, 195
ingenuity, 129
ingratitude, 129, 238–39
injuries, 129

injustice, 228
innocence, 102
insensitivity, 130
insinuating lies, 130. *See also* slander
insinuations, 216
insolence, 70
insurrection, 130, 201. *See also* rebellion
integrity, 40, 131. *See also* character
intelligence, 131
interest, 131–32, 182, 192, 205, 212, 213, 228
invading armies, 132, 245
invasion, 241
inveteracy, 183
irrational expressions, 132
irrationality, 133
irreconcilable disputes, 133
islanders: narrow perspective of, 53–54

jargon, 133
Jefferson, Thomas, 22, 24, 29–30, 31
Jesus Christ, 133, 162, 190, 198. *See also* Christianity
judgment, 127, 134; differs from genius, 105, 134. *See also* discretion; hasty judgments; prudence; reflection
jury trial, 134
justice, 135–36, 193, 195
justness, 136

kindness, 166
knowledge, 136–37, 165, 227; killed by schooling, 209; learned from misfortune and mistakes, 110, 153; man as a learner all of life, 191; scientific, 209; source of, 227. *See also* ignorance; wisdom

lack of follow through, 137
Lafayette, Marquis de, 18, 25, 41–42
Lambert, Mary, 3–4
land, 137; surveying, 210. *See also* agriculture; earth; farming; property
language, 137–38; misuse of words, 153; silence as a loud, 216; words help clarify thoughts, 227. *See also* writers; writing
languages, dead, 209

Laurens, Henry, 33
Laurens, John, 15
law, practice of, 106
law of nations, 138–39
law of nature, 139. *See also* bills of
rights; freedom; liberty; natural
rights
laws, 139–40; despots have nothing to
do with, 82; misapplication of, 190;
as sovereign, 201. *See also*
government
lawyers, 140–41
leadership, 141
learning, 191
Lee, Arthur, 20, 22
Lee, Richard Henry, 22
legislative tyranny, 141
Lewes, England, 4
liberty, 141–42; abuse of, 179, 190;
depends on obedience to laws, 140;
and humanity, 142. *See also* bills of
rights; freedom; law of nature;
natural rights
liberty of the press, 143. *See also*
magazines; newspapers
lies, 143–44, 166
life, shortness of, 215. *See also* death
little minds, 44
Livingston, Robert R., 17
Louis XVI, 26. *See also* France; French
Revolution
Louisiana Purchase, 31
love, 144
love of the people, 144
loyalty: of immigrants, 144–45
luxuries, 145
Luzerne, Chevalier de la, 21

McClenaghan, Blair, 12
Madison, James, 22, 26
magazines, 145
Mahomet, 199
majority rule, 130, 146
man: equality of, 90; at the age of fifty,
146; unity of, 162
manners, 45, 46, 147, 166, 182, 191
manufactures, 96
marriage, 147; of female friends, 147–48

Marshall, John, 23
meanly right, 183
meanness, 148, 209, 238–39
mechanics, 148
memory, 127, 149. *See also* forgetfulness
mercy, 149, 195
method, 149–50, 152
military bearing, 150
military command, 151. *See also* armies
mischief, 151
misers, 151, 171, 189. *See also* avarice
misery, 152; relief of, 58
misfortune, 152; learning from, 110,
153
mistake, learning from, 110, 153. *See
also* errors
misuse of words, 153
mixed government, 153. *See also* forms
of government
moderation, 154
monarchy, 7–8, 112, 120, 154–57, 200,
201; and courtiers, 72; require
ignorance for support, 86; Scripture
opposes, 100
Monroe, James, 27
moral goodness, 157–58, 195
moral justice, 172
morality, 195, 198, 205
Morris, Gouverneur, 12, 17, 26, 27
Morris, Lewis, 22
Morris, Robert, 11, 16–18, 20
Moses, 198
motivation, 158
movement of the human body, 159
Muhlenberg, John, 13
munificence, 114. *See also* benevolence;
philanthropy
mutual fear, 234
mutual love, 234
mysteries in nature, 163
mystery, 233

national character, 20, 159, 234
national honor, 20, 159–60
national reputation, 20, 160
national sins, 160
nationalism, 160
nations, 161; greatness of, 184

natural philosophy, 195
natural rights, 142, 161–63, 208; as
  foundation for civil rights, 52–53,
  61; government of our own as a, 67,
  110; jury trial as, 134; man born
  with, 90
nature, 129, 163. *See also* The Creation;
  earth; universe
navies, 164
navigation, 210
naysayers, 164
necessity, 165
neighbor, respect for, 86, 111
neutrality, 165
new discoveries, 165
New Orleans, 31
new thinking, 165
newspapers, 166. *See also* liberty of the
  press; magazines
Newton, Sir Isaac, 3, 54
Newtonian science, 43
nobility, 25, 47. *See also* aristocracy
nobly wrong, 183
nonsense, 166, 196

oaths, 166
obligation, 166
obedience, to majority rule, 146
obstinacy, 97, 167
old age, 111, 167. *See also* death
Ollive, Elizabeth, 4
Ollive, Samuel, 4
openness, 64, 168
opinion, 168–69, 182; change of, 56, 94,
  205, 206; freedom of, 130, 146, 233;
  memory necessary to form, 149
opportunism, 169
oppression, 169, 186; resistance to, 208.
  See also despotism; power; tyranny
order, 170
origins, 170. *See also* beginnings; The
  Creation

Paine, Frances Cocke, 2
Paine, Joseph, 2–3
Paine, Thomas: arrives in America, 4–5;
  antislavery writings, 6, 12, 217;
  birth, 2; as citizen of the world, 74,
183; complexity of, 1–2; criticism of,
  9–10, 11, 12, 15–16, 19, 23, 26;
  education, 3; elected to French
  National Convention, 26;
  imprisoned, 27; and iron bridge,
  23–24; as lobbyist for Congress and
  army, 16–18; marriage, 3–4; method
  of writing, 5–6, 32–33; mission to
  France, 15; edits *Pennsylvania
  Magazine*, 5–6; seeks pensions,
  20–22; returns to America, 28; room
  of described, 18–19; signs on
  privateers, 3; unkempt appearance,
  2, 15–16, 28–29, 32; will, 32; will of
  God, 75
panics, 170
paper money, 109
parenting, 171
partial reforms, 194
passion, 171, 189
past hardships, 171
patriotism, 150, 172
peace, 172–73; and form of government,
  100
Peale, Charles Willson, 31
Pennsylvania: bank of, 11–12;
  constitution of, 69; Paine as clerk of
  Assembly of, 12–13
Pennsylvania Magazine, 5–6
people, the: alarmed quickly, 173;
  despots try to break spirit of, 82; as
  government in America, 40; love of,
  144; sovereignty of, 69. *See also*
  democracy
persecution, 158, 198, 199, 224, 227
perseverance, 40, 72. *See also* going the
  full course
perspective, breadth of, 53–54
petitioning, 173
philanthropy, 134, 174; of Quakers, 190.
  See also benevolence; munificence
poetry, 144
political failures, 174
political parties, 69, 174–75, 221. *See
  also* factions
political rights, 172. *See also* civil rights;
  natural rights; rights
politicians, 193

politics, 175
popularity, 176. *See also* fame
positive construction, 176
posterity, 177; cannot be fettered, 66, 104; virtue of is not hereditary, 177
potential, 177
poverty, 111, 177–78, 244
power, 178–79; gives stability, 219; sovereignty must have, 219
practice, 100
prayer, 30, 179
precedents, 161, 179–80
predestination, 180
predictions, 181
prejudice, 46, 62, 135, 168, 181–82, 192, 206
preparation, 182
press, the, 182. *See also* liberty of the press; newspapers
pride, 183, 240
principles, 183–85; and charity, 58; forms grow out of, 100, 113; genius should not be given without, 104; to learn, 46; man cannot make, 210; moderation in, 154; versus political parties, 69, 174; and precedents, 180; prudence a substitute for, 187; pursued unto death, 44; and revolutions, 205, 206; revolution in, 45; scientific, 210–11; of society, 112; standing on, 48; versus temper, 226; and time, 229
printing, 186
procrastination, 44, 186
progress, 66, 187
property, 144, 186; protection of, 67, 78, 111, 186, 208. *See also* security
protection, 162; of commerce, 164; for citizens abroad, 187. *See also* defense; security
prudence, 110, 187. *See also* discretion; judgment
public character, 188
public debt, 188
Public Good, 14
public opinion, 188
public policy, 188
public service, 189

public spirit, 189
punishments, 190

Quakers, 190, 199; oppose books teaching languages, 3; oppose war, 83, 172
qualifications for officeholding, 191
quotations, 191

rage, 191. *See* anger
rancor, 226
Randolph, Edmund, 9
rashness, 191
reason, 94, 133, 168, 182, 192–93, 195, 205, 228; avarice beyond reach of, 49; and discover of God, 107; inferior to facts, 94; impossible to use with despots, 81; rebellion against, 193
reasonableness, 193
rebellion, 193; right of, 193. *See also* insurrection
rectitude, 131
Reed, Joseph, 14
reflection, 152, 168, 182, 227. *See also* judgment
reform, 152, 194
Reformation, 43
rejection, 194
religion, 195–96; America as asylum for, 43; freedom of, 67, 162, 199–200; to do good, 74. *See also* Bible; The Creation; Christianity; deism; deists; God; heaven; the hereafter; hell; Jesus Christ; Quakers; Scripture; Trinity
religious diversity, 197–98
religious establishment, 198–99
remoteness, 200
representation. *See* republican form of government
reproach, 194, 200
republican form of government, 19, 25, 154, 200–202
republican virtue, 202
reputation, 202
resignation to God's will, 179
resistance to oppression, 208

resolution, 203
responses, 203
retaliation, 203–4. *See also* revenge
retirement, 204
revelation, 211
revenge, 158, 204. *See also* retaliation
revolutions, 204–6; opportunities in,
    105. *See also* American Revolution;
    French Revolution; insurrection;
    rebellion; revolutions in thought;
    sovereignty
revolutions in thought, 206–7
rewards, 207
ridiculous. *See* sublime
right ideas, 207
rights, 172, 207–8; beginning of at the
    Creation, 162, 180; of minors, 208;
    become duty by reciprocity, 86; from
    one generation to another, 104;
    security of, 111, 186. *See also* bills of
    rights
Rights of Man, 25–26
Rittenhouse, David, 7
rogues, 208
Romans, 41
rotation in office, 208–9
rules, 209
Rush, Benjamin, 6, 7, 8, 10, 28, 31, 32

satire, 209
science, 54, 96, 167, 209–10; as
    foundation for the arts, 48, 51; as
    foundation of theology, 73; God as
    creator of, 108; has its own
    language, 133; mechanics of, 148
scientific knowledge, 209
scientific principles, 210–11
Scripture, 190, 203, 210, 211–12;
    institutes no form of government,
    100. *See also* Bible; The Creation;
    God; religion
seafaring, 212
secrecy, 64, 123, 194
secrets, 212
security, 100, 162, 208, 212, 231. *See also*
    property; protection
seduction, 127
self-determination, 213

self-evident truths, 213
self-fulfilling prophesies, 213
self-interest, 214. *See also* interest
self-preservation, 214
self-respect, 214
sexual excess, 215
sharing burdens, 215
shipbuilding, 215
Short, William, 26
shortness of life, 215. *See also* death;
    old age
show of spirit, 37
sickness of thought, 46
silence, 56, 71, 216
simplicity, 216
slander, 216–17. *See also* insinuating lies
slavery, 6, 12, 217
smuggling, 217
social compact, 112, 146. *See also* law
    of nature; natural rights; state of
    nature
society versus government, 218–19
sovereignty, 219; laws as, 201; must
    have power, 219. *See also*
    revolution, right of
sovereignty of the people, 69
Spain, 8
stability, 219
state of nature, 220. *See also* law of
    nature; social compact
staying the course, 109, 220. *See also*
    perseverance
stories, 220
strange bedfellows, 221
strong, prey on weak, 83
study, 221
sublime, 221
submission, 221
sudden changes, 222
suffrage, 25, 222
suggestions, 223
suitability, 223
supposition, 223
surprise, 223
surveying, land, 210
suspicion, 65, 102, 224
sycophants, 47
sympathy, 224

talents, 205, 225
tariff, 225
taxes, 13, 80, 96, 113, 225–26, 242
temper, 75, 154, 226
temperance, 118
theology, 60, 73, 226–27
thinking, 227; habit of right, 207
thinking alike, 227
Thomas, Isaiah, 5–6
thought, freedom of, 174
thoughts, 138, 187, 227–28. *See also* ideas
time, 107, 122, 131, 192, 228; and principles, 229
times that try/tried men's souls, 11, 19, 45, 75
titles, 229
tolerance, 30, 229
toleration, 230
trade, 230. *See also* commerce
treachery, 55, 231
treason, 231
treaties, 99, 159, 231. *See also* peace; war
treaties of peace, 232
triangle, principle of, 210–11
trigonometry, 210
trinity, 108
truth, 184, 229, 232–33
types of men, 233
tyranny, 11, 121, 185, 199, 233–34; legislative, 141; rebellion against, 193

unicameralism, 8, 23, 234
union, 234
unity, 234
universe, 3, 163, 235–36; as the bible, 196; endlessness of, 107, 234
unjust measures, 237
ups and downs, 237
usefulness, 221
usurpation, 237. *See also* despotism; tyranny

valor, 237. *See also* bravery; courage; cowardice
vanity, 238

Vergennes, Comte de, 15
vice, 209, 238–39
victory, 239
vigor, 239
virtue, 46, 135, 182, 183, 195; not hereditary, 177, 239. *See also* constitutional amendments
volunteerism, 240
voting, 240. *See also* suffrage

war, 159, 240–43; and form of government, 100; Quakers oppose, 83; weakness in, 243. *See also* disarmament; enemies; treaties; treaties of peace
war profiteers, 243
Ward, Samuel, 9
Washington, George, 9, 11, 13, 15, 16–17, 19, 21, 22, 25, 26, 27
Watson, Elkanah, 15–16
weak: become prey of strong, 83; in war, 243
wealth, 244; and avarice, 49
weapons, 245. *See also* disarmament
Whitney, Eli, 28–29
wicked, 120. *See also* evils
wisdom, 97, 189, 245. *See also* ignorance; knowledge
wishes, 246
wit, 246. *See also* satire
women, 246
word of God. *See* Bible; The Creation; Scripture
"world-makers," 72. *See also* The Creation
writers, 140, 247
writing, 247. *See also* language; poetry; satire
wrong and right, 183, 247. *See also* bad and good
wrongs, 248. *See also* errors; mistake

youth, 248

zealots, 248. *See also* fanaticism
zealousness, 248